A
Savior
for All
Seasons

BY *William P. Barker*

Everyone in the Bible
Tarbell's Teacher's Guide

A Savior for All Seasons

William P. Barker

Fleming H. Revell Company
Old Tappan, New Jersey

Library of Congress Cataloging-in-Publication Data

Barker, William Pierson.
  A Savior for all seasons.

  1. Jesus Christ—Person and offices. 2. Christian
life—1960–   . I. Title.
BT202.B32   1986   232'.3   86-6648
ISBN 0-8007-1485-7

Copyright © 1986 by William P. Barker
Published by the Fleming H. Revell Company
Old Tappan, New Jersey 07675
All rights reserved
Printed in the United States of America

To
Bill,
Stefan,
John,
Peter,
Andreas,
and
Bradley
❦

Contents

Preface

"For everything there is a season," the old sage of the Hebrew scriptures observed (Ecclesiastes 3:1).

"For every season, there is a Savior," every son and daughter of the New Covenant can respond.

Jesus Christ is Lord of all life. The risen, living One marches as a fellow pilgrim with us through every season of our lives. His promise holds: He bestows life in the midst of every set of circumstances. He gives us new beginnings when we see only dismal endings. Jesus Christ is the Savior for *all* seasons.

This is not pious preacher talk. This is the promise of the New Testament, backed by the claim of the Christian community for nearly 2,000 years and reiterated by the whispers

of the Holy Spirit this moment. The conviction that Jesus
Christ is Savior for all seasons has become increasingly real
and important to me through serving as a pastor for over
thirty-five years. This is not theory to me; it is certainty born
of experience. Each of the "seasons" described in the following chapters has been experienced personally, and each season has been hallowed by the awareness that Jesus Christ has
encountered me there.

So many people have had a part in putting together these
chapters that I risk omitting key people when I list names. I
must express a special word of appreciation to members of
the church family at Allentown and to staff colleagues, Mrs.
Susan Eltringham, the Reverend Wilbur E. Goist, Mrs. Deb-
orah Palmer, Mrs. Gloria Snyder, the Reverend John K.
Stoner and the Reverend Susan Pizor Yoder, who patiently
serve with me to "preach the word, be urgent in season and
out of season . . ." (2 Timothy 4:2). Fred M. Rogers and the
Luxor Ministerial Association have given constant counsel.
Sandy and John Barker and Ellen and Martin Brutsch have
helped me to know that Jesus Christ is truly the Savior for all
persons for all life's seasons. Jean, partner in pilgrimage for
over thirty-five years of marriage, has experienced each season with me and sustained me with her love and prayers. Finally, I owe Mrs. Patricia Fainor an enormous debt of
gratitude for patiently typing and preparing this manuscript.

WILLIAM P. BARKER
Allentown, Pennsylvania

1

He Speaks to Us
As Friend to Friend

Few of us are hermits. Some of us may live alone, many may be lonely, but almost none of us exist in solitude, totally isolated from others like a Carmelite nun.

We are in some sort of community with other humans some of the time: a marriage, a dormitory, a barracks or a ship's company. It may be the eight-to-five gang you work with, or the class you take on Tuesday nights, or the bowling team—but you do interact with other people part of each day.

Being with others does not necessarily mean that it is easy to get along with them, however. And human relationships surely form one of the most challenging areas of life. Some people, sadly, let that challenge get the best of them. French actress Brigitte Bardot, a semirecluse after years of being typecast as a sex kitten, shuns people. "I hate humanity; I am allergic to it," she states emphatically. "I find my equilibrium in nature, in the company of animals."

She is not alone. Author Colin Cherry had three successive editions of a book published. In the first edition, Dr. Cherry dedicated the book: "To my dog, Pym." In the second edition, Dr. Cherry wrote the following inscription: "To all those human beings who have inquired so kindly after my dog, Pym." When the third edition was prepared, the author had the following words placed on the dedication page: "To the memory of my dog, Pym." Curiously, Cherry's book carries the title *On Human Condition*.

All this suggests that Professor Cherry focused a lot of affection on his dog. There is nothing wrong with caring for canines, of course, but let's hope that pups don't push aside people in our priorities. Pym might have been a special pal, but humans are more special. There is a theological aspect, too! Life is meant to be lived with an awareness of other people.

The Bible opens with God's wanting to be in community. The Lord created the "earthling" (the literal Hebrew meaning of *Adam*). God did not intend His earthling creation to exist apart from a community. "Then the Lord God said, 'It is not good that the man should be alone . . .' " (Genesis 2:18). God wills community. The Creator plans for humans to live with others, sharing their lives with one another.

God is absorbed in the needs of living persons. Throughout the Bible, especially through Jesus Christ, He has demonstrated that He makes His decision to bring life. We are Christ's people, and we are given life to share with others. No matter how brilliant we may be or how successful we may appear, if we fail to decide to use our lives to give life to others, we have not fulfilled God's will for us.

It's Hard to Live With Others

Julia Ward Howe, the great reformer and writer, once asked Senator Charles Sumner if she could introduce him to the famous actor Edwin Booth. Senator Sumner haughtily declined, muttering, "I have outlived my interest in individuals." Julia Ward Howe often recalled Sumner's refusal and later remarked, "Fortunately, God Almighty has never gotten that far."

She could have added that the Lord God Almighty never *will* get that far! He assures each of us that He is intensely interested in us individually. He gives us the rich satisfaction of knowing that we are loved, *regardless!* And He impels each of us to have a satisfying interest in others as persons!

We may agree with this idea in theory, but we quickly discover that the real world means trying to relate to people who are less than perfect.

For several years, I served as a leader of seminars for young pastors who had been ordained three to five years earlier. Studies had shown that the highest dropout rate among ministers occurred among those in that category, and the seminars were designed to assist pastors over this crisis period. They all were serving in parish ministry. They were all very angry people. Their anger sprayed over everything—anger toward the institutional church for getting them into situations they found difficult to cope with; anger toward the seminaries for not preparing them better for the real world; anger toward their spouses for not being more supportive; anger toward God for allowing them to be hurt; anger toward themselves for being angry. Mostly, however, their anger seemed to be vented toward their congregations.

One afternoon, one young pastor heatedly denounced his church. He excoriated the usher who showed up with boozy breath. He scolded the officers who showed no initiative. He condemned those who accused him of being communistic every time he spoke on social justice issues. He branded the parents who dropped off their children for Sunday school and sat in their cars reading the paper. After the pastor finally finished his scathing indictment of nearly everyone in his congregation, he was red in the face and speaking through clenched teeth. "I am ready to write off the church," he announced. "In fact," he added emphatically, "I'm ready to write off the whole lousy human race!"

A long silence followed. Then someone quietly asked if this might not also be the way that God could feel about everyone, including preachers. The angry young pastor looked startled.

Isn't this the problem that God has with all of us? Yet He has not written us off! God has not quit on us. He has given His solemn word that He continues to relate to us in love. The One who hung on the cross is God's assurance that He insists on "hanging in there" with us.

We Reduce Others to Clichés

Some clichés go with the territory. Every funeral director secretly winces when hearing the tired cracks: "I hear your business is dying." "You'll be the last to let me down." What barber has not endured jibes about being the "town cut-up"? Every law-enforcement officer will encounter people who dismiss him or her as a "dumb cop." No matter how honest and honorable, a professional realtor or automobile dealer will be accused of being a "shyster" or "operator" or "high-pressure salesman." Every young person has squirmed and seethed from being made to feel he or she is "just a dumb kid" or "a mixed-up teenager." Women who are deliberately choosing to serve as homemakers resent the tone and implications of being labeled "only a housewife."

In each case, these humans are dismissed by a throwaway line. Clichés make them feel like disposable persons.

My brother-in-law is an engineer with Westinghouse, de-

signing and selling nuclear power plants. He attended a
church in Massachusetts one summer and introduced himself
to another worshiper. Hearing my brother-in-law's line of
work, the recently introduced stranger snapped the words,
"Death merchant!" turned on his heel and walked away.
Killed by a cliché, my brother-in-law could only shake his
head.

In Robert Penn Warren's novel *The Cave* one of the characters is known in the town as "the Greek," or "Nick, the
Greek," or sometimes merely as the guy who runs the lunch
stand. One day a woman speaks to him, addressing him by
his name and calling him "Mister Papadoupolos." The dignity of being known by his name almost brings the man to
tears.

In John 4, Jesus meets a woman who wants to think of Him
as a cliché and expects Him to treat her as a vulgar cliché.
She refers to Him as "Jew" and to herself as "Samaritan."
There it is: all neatly packaged, marked and shelved. The relationship is reduced to an exchange of trite comments, if she
has her way.

Jesus, however, refuses to let the matter rest. He will not
refer to her as a cliché. She persists in flirtatious cliché talk
with Jesus, but Jesus insists on seeing her as a sister instead of
a stereotype.

God also sees you as a person—a special person—never as
a cliché. He sees past all the labels. He ignores all categories.
He knows you for the sometimes lonely, sometimes anxious,
sometimes angry person you are, yet He never dismisses you
with a demeaning description. He insists on speaking to you
as Friend to friend. You may think your life is commonplace,
but He says you are never common.

In a world that tries to think of you and others as stereo-
types, God in Christ finds fresh, vital expressions to describe
the relationship He means to enjoy with you. Will you see
yourself through His eyes? Will you see yourself as a per-

son who is unique and who can never be sloughed off with a cliché?

Knowing that God never sees you as a stereotype, will you see others as persons rather than functions? Those you associate with, especially those you live with, are human beings who want to be more than conveniences or appliances in life. Nonetheless, do you take them for granted?

Being Taken for Granted

One mother, tired of being taken for granted as the drudge constantly picking up after her two sons, decided to put an end to it once and for all. For every item she had to pick up from the floor of their constantly disorderly room, she said they would have to pay her a nickel. At the end of the week, the boys owed her sixty-five cents. She put a note on their dressers and sighed with relief, thinking this would teach them an important lesson. She received payment promptly in an envelope on the kitchen table—along with a fifty-cent tip and a note that read, "Thanks, Mom. Keep up the good work!"

We often overlook the fact that Jesus was almost constantly surrounded by people. No hermit on a mountaintop in perpetual solitary meditation, He lived with others. Astonishingly, He never took any other person for granted. Look at the many times lepers and beggars intruded, yet He refused to dismiss them as nuisances. He never saw them as part of the scenery; He regarded each as a person.

Remember the pathetic woman with the bleeding condition that had weakened her, rendered her ceremonially unclean and taken all her savings in doctor's bills? Others take her for granted as a hopeless invalid, a chronic nuisance. She timidly touches the fringe on Jesus' prayer shawl or robe. Jesus does not take for granted that this is merely one more problem or sick person, but a woman needing healing.

Jesus never takes you for granted. This is the meaning of

the Gospel in this age when so many take you for granted: You are a person whom He knows and loves as special in His life.

Several years ago, during a census, a census taker called at an apartment in a teemingly crowded part of Detroit. A woman came to the door holding a baby, with five other children clinging to her. The census taker started his questions, and soon came to the one asking, "And how many children do you have?"

The woman carefully answered, "Well, there is Debbie Sue, there is Jimmy, there is Tracy Lynne, there's Beth Anne, there is. . . ."

The census taker impatiently cut her off. "Forget the names, lady. Just give me the number."

The woman's eyes blazed. "In *this* home, the children are *not* numbers. They are names!" she replied indignantly.

Through Jesus Christ, we understand that we are not mere numbers but are names known and loved by God.

Two Italian artists portrayed the Last Supper. Each painted with the strokes of a master. One picture of the Last Supper was rendered by Andrea del Castagno at the Santa Maria della Grazie at Milan. The other is the well-known version by Leonardo da Vinci. Why has "The Last Supper" by da Vinci remained a favorite with everyone, including the experts? Art critics say that del Castagno's "Last Supper" reveals near-flawless brushwork and a magnificent attention to the details of the background. But that is exactly why da Vinci's painting excels. Leonardo da Vinci sketched the figures first and fit the background to them. With Andrea del Castagno, it was the other way around: He worked on the background first and fit the figures into it. Da Vinci concentrated on the people; consequently, they appear larger than life. They appear animated.

The mark of a master, whether in painting or in living, is the intention to put people first and then fit the background to them. Jesus did this in His relationships; we respond by doing the same in ours, especially for those with whom we live.

The home resembling a Norman Rockwell painting is a rarity. More than 60 percent of all mothers with children under eighteen now hold jobs; nearly half of all marriages end in divorce; more than a fourth of all families (up from 13 percent in 1970) are headed by single parents; fewer than 10 percent of all families are traditional. Traditional families are defined as father at work and mother at home with two children.

Whatever the pattern of your family, traditional or nontraditional, you are called as Christ's person to put other people first as persons.

A home built at the corner of Lexington Avenue and Eighty-second Street in New York City in 1882 was only five feet wide at each end. This odd-shaped structure was erected because the builder-owner, Joseph Richardson, was determined to spite the owner of an adjacent apartment house. Richardson could not forgive the apartment owner for a minor annoyance and lived in his "spite house" from 1882 until his death fifteen years later.

The Art of Listening

Do you sometimes live in a spite house? As a husband or a wife, as a father or a mother, as a son or a daughter, are you making your home a colony of heaven or an outpost of hell? Do you exist in a state of uneasy truce with the others in your family? Are you wary and uncommunicative with them?

Seven out of every ten minutes of the working day are spent communicating. Seventy percent of your conscious working time! Of that, 9 percent is spent in writing, 16 percent in reading, 30 percent in talking, and 45 percent in listening.

The problem is in the listening. Although you spend 45

percent of communication time listening, if you are typical, you operate at only about a 25 percent level of efficiency in listening.

United Airlines once had an airline employee stand at an arrival gate at Kennedy Airport in New York and repeat over and over to disembarking passengers, "Welcome to Dubuque." Not one of the passengers took any note of the fact that he might be getting off at the wrong city!

Listening is largely a lost art. Perhaps it's because we live under such a barrage of messages and noises that we must screen out most. We hear but do not listen.

Leopold Stokowski used to complain that few people listen to orchestra music. They would come up to him after a concert and say, "I saw you conduct the [such and such] orchestra." They saw; they did not listen.

We are terrible at listening, but, incredibly, we make few attempts to improve our listening skills. If we do, we search for a gimmick, a device. With all the discussions about that overworked word *communication*, courses in communications are almost invariably in speaking and writing effectively. Rarely is anything said about listening.

About the only ones doing much listening today are the psychiatrists, psychologists, a few in the mental health field, and occasionally a pastor who has had some specialized pastoral-care training. People are so hungry to have someone listen to them that they will call for appointments and pay fees to many counselors.

Do you sometimes wish that someone would listen—*really listen*—to you?

God Listens

The writers of Scripture knew that God is *the* listener. They showed it was more than a case of God tuning in on prayers, since God does not prick up His ears only at pious talk. Quite the reverse; He seems bored by or even annoyed at our unctuous, wordy speeches that we try to pawn off as praying. However, He always listens. Psalms 102:18–22 describes how God hears the groans of prisoners. God is able to detect the faintest signals for help from a hurting man or woman. He can instantly decode the groans and sobs of unarticulated prayers when a person knows he needs the Lord's help (*see* Romans 8:26–28).

Jesus was the master listener. The more you become acquainted with Him as He is disclosed in the Gospel accounts, the more you become aware of His listening skills. His interviews with people are superb case histories of listening.

Here strides the rich young ruler. He has wealth, power, recognition: two cars, a boat, a cabin in the mountains. He sits on three boards, heads his own company, has been voted outstanding man of the year.

Jesus listens.

Behind all the words from the rich young ruler is a plea. Something is missing. "Is this all there is to life? Making a bunch and having everyone shake my hand? So what if I have two new Mercedes in the driveway? So what if I head a global conglomerate and keep my yachts in Corfu and St. Tropez and fly my private jet weekends to the Caribbean?"

Jesus listens. He catches the messages. Yes, Jesus hears how respectable and decent the man is. "But one thing you still lack."

The man knows Jesus has been listening and replies, "What's that?"

"Sell all you have, give to the poor, and come follow me."

Jesus is listening to you. He hears the tiny voices inside you that you may not even listen to. Jesus helps you to listen to those voices. He enables you to listen to others.

In fact, there is a section of the Pentecost story in Acts 2 which always fascinates me because of the repeated references to the way the coming of the Holy Spirit opened communication among people. They heard one another! They listened to one another! The speaking in tongues might have been the manifestation of something similar to the charismatic movement, but I think it also refers to listening. The Spirit enabled them to listen with love to others. ". . . each one heard them speaking in his own language" (Acts 2:6).

The Spirit of Christ gave them the miracle of being able to listen with compassion. Theodore Reik speaks of listening with what he calls the "third ear," that is with an ear of sensitivity, an ear of caring, with the empathetic ear. James writes, "Let every man be quick to hear, slow to speak . . ." (James 1:19).

The more you are Christ's, the more you are able to hear others in their native language. Acts 2 presents a long list of various languages that were represented at Pentecost. Let's add some others.

What about what Haim Ginnott calls "Childrenese"—the language that children speak? Many parents do not seem to know this language any longer. "Hey, Mom, look what I just drew," is more than an invitation to look at a crayoned masterpiece; it is also a call for reassurance and a request to be taken seriously. "Hey, Dad, let's play football!" is not expressing a desire to be coached to perfection as a major leaguer; it is a plea for closeness.

Children speak in symbols. As parents, we have to decode those symbols into plain language, then respond. "Look what I just drew" is not a message asking for a critique of the artwork. Only the mother or father who has learned to listen in love can hear what is really being said.

What is the comment made most frequently by American fathers to their children? A survey of children by Dr. and Mrs. Delmar W. Holbrook, directors of the family counseling service of the Seventh Day Adventist Church, reports that most children hear their fathers telling them they are too tired to do anything with them or for them.

"We don't have enough money," was found to be the second most used comment of fathers, followed by "Keep quiet!"

What are the remarks most frequently heard by those in your home? Parenthood demands more than a spate of complaints and commands to children.

Sometimes we tune out the signals from our children because they mean listening to some voices from our own childhood. These may be voices we don't want to hear, painful memories of our own childhood, when we were pleading to be heard but no one understood. Now, instead of trying to listen to our own children, we may feel only our own pain, which we would rather not remember.

Listening—A Form of Love

I used to be puzzled when I was tired after an afternoon of hearing people's problems. Then I learned the physiological aspects of listening. I found that listening literally demands increased energy. The heart speeds up. The blood circulates faster. The body temperature goes up. Listening is an activity. Listening is hard.

Listening with love to others is what Martin Buber calls the "I-Thou" relationship. This is not the "I-It" relationship. Listening with love changes the relationship from "I-It" to "I-Thou."

Look at your marriage from this perspective. How much are you listening to your partner?

A young, newly transferred corporation man tells me, "I cannot figure out my wife. She has everything—nice home, every appliance, good neighborhood, even a new car at her disposal. I don't run around or drink or beat the kids or kick the dog. But we just don't seem to communicate anymore."

Translated, this man's words mean: "I do not try to listen." His wife is saying, "I have no meaningful relationships outside my home. I am lonely. I am not accepted here yet." The husband is not using his spiritual scanner to detect those signals. He is not listening with love.

A woman who had been married for many years was suddenly confronted by her husband, who announced that he
was leaving her to continue his affair with another woman.
The wife felt deep pain. When she talked with her pastor, she
said, "What hurts me most is not that he slept with her or
that he gave her jewelry, but that he had something to *talk
about* with her."

We have been led to believe that intimacy can take care of
everything in marriage, especially bedroom intimacy. This is
a fallacy. Listening with love is the beginning of meaningful
relationships.

I am dismayed when I talk with couples planning marriage
or having marital problems who have read extensively on the
mechanics of lovemaking and assume they have all the
knowledge they will need to make a marriage succeed.
Studying articles and books on the physiology and psychol-
ogy of sex will not mean a growing relationship. In fact, the
emphasis on the erotic in our culture leads husbands and
wives to treat each other as pleasure machines to be adjusted
and manipulated. It is not how much you *know*, but how
much you *love* in marriage.

The writer Balzac told of a husband who knew everything.
The man was a brilliant research chemist. He was so totally
absorbed in his scientific research that he ignored his wife
and treated her as a machine to be operated for his convenience. One day while describing a part of his latest experi-
ment, he noticed his wife was crying.

"Tears," he said suddenly. "I have analyzed tears. Tears
contain a little phosphate of lime, chloride of sodium, mucus,
and water."

He knew everything, and yet he knew nothing. He saw this
woman he was married to as everything *except* a person.
Caring is more important than knowing!

Caring is listening, and listening is taking the other
seriously. Listening with love is allowing the other person to

become. It is the opposite of obliterating the other. When you are listening with love, you are accepting this person just as he or she is. The full depth of the other person's being is heard. The ultimate welfare of the other person is the listener's final concern, and this helps allow God to bring wholeness.

Are you listening with love to your spouse?

Love begins for you and me with what God has done.

Because of what God has done, you and I as husbands and wives now do for each other. It does not depend upon whims of emotion. It does not rely on how lovable the other is. "Beloved, if God so loved us, we also ought to love one another" (1 John 4:11).

Love, then, is not the gland-stirring passion generated by a shapely nymph and a macho millionaire. Love is the smile a paunchy, balding husband offers when his wife, in hair curlers and a faded dressing gown, has managed to burn the toast for the thousandth time in twenty years of marriage.

Historian Will Durant recalled his parents' happy marriage in spite of poverty and hardship. Durant particularly liked to remember the way his mother smiled fondly at her French-Canadian woodcutter husband as she passed the food around the table on their fiftieth wedding anniversary. "I thank God for giving me this old man to take care of," she stated.

How many marriages are built on this kind of gratitude to God? Old Madame Durant, in her simple peasant faith, uttered the profoundest truth about Christian marriage: A true partnership between a husband and wife grows when each thanks God for having the other to take care of. This is love!

Love, then, is not the sappy sentimentalism of a Sir Lancelot sighing over a glistening young Guinevere. Love is a weary middle-aged husband coming home, putting a casserole in the oven and setting the table again because his working wife has missed her bus for the twentieth night in a row.

Love is not the erotic thrills of a romantic Romeo serenading a nubile Juliet by moonlight. Love is going to the symphony with her when he would have better enjoyed a football game.

Love is not the romanticism of a Prince Charming wanting to marry only the Cinderella with a foot small enough to fit into his glass slipper. It is the man who knows his wife wears a size 10B and that her feet hurt and make her cranky sometimes.

Love is not soft music and sweet words. Love is not a constant round of candy, flowers and anniversary presents. Love is a long series of sacrifices: the hunting trip that gives way to a new washer; a new party dress and dream cruise that give way to braces; the evening out for dinner and a show that gives way to shoes for the children.

A young girl, noticing her mother working over the sink cleaning up the pots and pans from dinner, asked, "How can you stand doing dishes day after day?"

The mother smiled and looked up. "I'm not washing dishes, Jennifer. I'm building a home!"

That kind of discipline and devotion reflects the love of God through Jesus Christ. And that kind of love is the way you act when you live with others.

2

We Walk Alone Until We Walk With Jesus

On May 22, 1913, the liner *Cedric* was ready to sail from Liverpool to New York. People lined the decks and docks waving farewells. Everyone seemed to have friends to call and wave good-bye to. Everyone, that is, except the poet Rupert Brooke. In spite of the crowds and music, he felt desolate. Noticing a ragged boy loitering on the dock, Brooke raced down the gangplank just before the ship's whistle blew. He found the boy and learned the youngster's name was William. "Will you wave to me if I give you sixpence?" Brooke asked.

Moments later, the gangways were lowered, the lines cast

off. The whistles blew and tugs eased the liner away from the dock. Handkerchiefs and hats waved. The band played. People called farewells. Among the crowd on the pier was a little lad named William, clutching his sixpence, straining his eyes across the widening gap of water and vigorously waving a ragged bandanna. Later Rupert Brooke immortalized the scene in a poem: "And so I got me sixpen'orth and my farewell—dear William," the lonely poet wrote. Surrounded by people, Brooke was alone. In his loneliness, the poet wanted someone to think of him, even if he had to pay for it.

We are all alone. Even while others are with us, each of us stands alone. Like trees in the forest, the branches may intertwine and mingle with others, but the trunk stands alone. It must send its own roots into the soil, must seek out its own nourishment. Each person, like each tree, ultimately stands alone.

Do you remember that *Peanuts* cartoon where Linus is afraid to go to the library and Charlie Brown tries to explain that everyone is lonely in some place or another? Linus, in turn, asks Charlie where that place is for him.

Charlie ponders that one, then replies, "Earth."

Loneliness vs. Aloneness

Loneliness and aloneness are not the same. *Loneliness* is the pain of being alone. *Aloneness* is the glory of being alone. Most of us experience the ache of loneliness. Only a few have learned to savor the significance of solitude. Those who can glory in being alone on occasion are the saint or poet or explorer.

Charles A. Lindbergh knew this kind of aloneness when he soloed across the Atlantic in 1927. Years later, Lindbergh wrote to Michael Collins, who piloted *Apollo II* while fellow astronauts Neil Armstrong and Edwin Aldrin made their historic moon walk. Lindbergh knew the aloneness Collins had felt in the command module orbiting toward the back side of the moon, where he was utterly cut off from the earth: "You have experienced aloneness unknown to man before," Lindbergh told Collins, "but I believe you will find that it lets you think and sense with a greater clarity."

The aloneness that offers that kind of perspective is healthy. However, you more often experience loneliness as the pain of being alone.

Loneliness comes in many shades. Loneliness may be colored light blue, or dull gray, or deep black. Loneliness also comes in various shapes. Some loneliness has sharp, jagged edges. Some weighs so much that when it tilts onto you, it's too heavy to move.

Loneliness is when you have recently moved to a new community. Loneliness is being a corporation gypsy. (At one time, IBM people claimed the firm's initials stood for "I've Been Moved.") But the term *corporation gypsy* or *company Bedouin* does not quite apply, because with the gypsies and the Bedouins, the entire community shifts residence. You are alone. You have been torn from your old relationships. You have been uprooted from the familiar people and places you knew. You no longer have the security and stability of the old community.

Loneliness is going away to college or into the armed forces. Loneliness is being eighteen to twenty-two years old, and, like half of those in that age bracket, being away from home. Loneliness is being in your teens. Counselors will tell you that this is one of the loneliest times of your life. In *Up the Down Staircase*, Bel Kaufman drew a portrait of a Puerto Rican boy in a big, inner-city high school. No one remembered that his name was José Rodriguez, so when he dropped notes into the suggestion box, he signed them merely "me." One day, a piece of paper with the signature "me" appeared in the suggestion box, wishing himself a happy birthday. Nobody knew—or cared—about José's birthday.

Loneliness is bearing responsibility. Loneliness is when you must make decisions affecting others. Loneliness is being an executive. "The Presidency of the United States is the loneliest job in the world," Harry Truman insisted. You, however, privately feel that your job matches Harry's for loneliness.

Loneliness is when your children all leave home. Loneliness is when your fiancé is sent overseas. Loneliness is when you start to withdraw into yourself and shut others out. Life can easily become all mirrors and no windows.

Loneliness is being a single parent or widow. You are an exile. You are tired of well-meaning friends or family members who seem to think that if you would remarry, you would be happy. You are suspicious of acquaintances who invite you to dinner and scheme to match you up with a possible mate. You resent those old friends who used to invite you and your spouse but now seem to shun you because you're single. You are incensed by those people who assume that because you are single, you're sexually available.

Loneliness is being unemployed and feeling like a piece of useless junk on life's rubbish pile. Loneliness is being forced to take early retirement because of health or a company merger or a plant shutdown. Loneliness is knowing that you are a surplus commodity. Loneliness is the indignity and frustration of being unneeded.

Loneliness is feeling abandoned in a society that worships youth. Loneliness is sitting in a rocker in a time that regards old age as a disgrace. Loneliness comes from realizing that you can no longer compete in a world that idolizes sports and sex. Loneliness is when a prolonged illness, a stroke or a broken hip makes your body degenerate and your appearance change. Loneliness is when your wheelchair is pushed in front of the television to endure another long day of silly serials and game shows.

The worst form of loneliness—*the* loneliest spot in the world—is when your life partner is dead. Bereavement is so awful that no words exist that adequately portray the state.

This type of loneliness is as close to unbearable as the feelings of an infant who thinks itself deserted. In fact, psychiatrists point out that tiny babies whose mothers have died show the same evidence of depression that older people do in grief.

"No man is an island," wrote poet John Donne. Yet in a sense each of us is. There are rooms in your heart where no one has ever walked. You may long to usher in others, but no one will ever come. No one can.

Popular Antidotes Against Loneliness

"Throw yourself into your job," advise some. This is the theory that loneliness is simply an unused or unfilled block of time. "Fill the void and loneliness will disappear."

Although there is a therapeutic quality to work, merely being busy is no cure-all for loneliness. "When I get home to my apartment after a hectic day, I still have to face the fact that there's only lonely old me to eat the TV dinner with," sighed one single.

"Have some fun!" others tell you. Dancing, bowling, clubs and parties, however, can become activities to mask loneliness. Industries exploiting boredom and catering to the lonely offer things to do and places to go, but none relieve loneliness.

"Get a girl."

"Find a man."

Our eroticized culture insists that the way to relieve loneliness is to give way to lust. Pop psychologists leave the impression that the cure for loneliness is to have a meaningful sexual relationship. The frantic search for the right partner or bigger kicks merely brings greater isolation. The most lonely, haunted man is the office wolf. Persons indulging in romantic affairs are cannibals devouring each other to ease the hunger for authentic relationships. How many marriages are undertaken because one or both partners expects the other to take away the loneliness? Those who imagine that intimacy means the end of loneliness will find the relationship doomed. Lone-liness will not be abolished merely by sharing a bedroom with another.

"Be with others! Socialize. Get out with people," urge others.

Lady Ottoline Morrell was one of England's great host-esses. She entertained the cream of society at her country home during World War I. Any given weekend, her guests might have included such names as Bertrand Russell, D.H. Lawrence, Aldous Huxley, Katherine Mansfield, Siegfried Sassoon, and Prime Minister Asquith. Her home rang with the voices of the great. In all of this conviviality, she still complained in her diaries of intense loneliness. "Here I sit," she wrote, "with all these people and talk and talk, yet we all remain outside each other and never really blend and live to-gether, as the flowers do. How inaccessible we all are!"

"Perhaps another drink will help," others tell you.

Poet Roy Helton correctly calls liquor "lonesome water." Cocktails or cocaine or any other chemical crutch may deaden the pain of the isolated person for a time, but the bottle builds a glass wall between that person and others. In fact, one of the symptoms of alcoholism is intense loneliness, even panic, in a crowd.

"Pull yourself together. Be self-reliant. Stand on your own two feet," counsel many.

Loneliness can be an appalling depressant. For all his rig-orous navy training and lofty motivation, six months in the Antarctic threw famed polar explorer Admiral Richard E. Byrd into a state of depression. His book *Alone* describes the ordeal of loneliness during a winter at the South Pole, where discipline and determination proved to be poor props against the weight of loneliness.

"Poor me." Pity yourself. Dwell on the fact that you are not someone else, or that you haven't earned the respect and love of others. Is this your way of handling loneliness?

Never Lonely Again

We will be lonely until we accept the Companion. We walk alone—until we walk with Jesus.

If we put our trust in crowds, in work, in leisure, in lovers or in anything except Him, we will know loneliness. There is no substitute. Even marriage, church, hobbies, good causes, family or interesting jobs will be merely a means of marking time. No matter how much company or how little, we are forsaken without the right Company.

Jesus should have been the loneliest man of all. John the Baptist was perplexed by Him. The disciples were puzzled by Him. Even His own family, who were mistaken about the sick He healed, were confused. Government leaders and religious authorities all suspected Him. His closest friends let Him down. They slept at Gethsemane when asked to sit up with Him. Judas betrayed him. Peter denied Him. His enemies plotted against Him. The crowds shouted for His death. The thief dying with Him ridiculed Him. The bystanders taunted Him.

Nobody understood Him. Nobody honored Him. Nobody welcomed Him. Nobody loved Him. Nobody wanted Him. Yet He was never lonely!

The evening of His arrest, Jesus calmly announced, "The hour is coming, indeed it has come, when you will be scattered, every man to his home, and will leave me alone; yet I am not alone, for the Father is with me" (John 16:32).

Psychiatrists' studies show that much unrecognized loneliness is really grief over the loss of a parent, a playmate, a toy, a friend—any childhood ally that was indispensable for survival. This is a way of saying that the real cause of loneliness is separation from God.

You and I have turned from Him. We have wanted to go our own ways; now we are apprehensive. We see ony death, futility and meaninglessness, assuming we are alone. But our loneliness is actually a result of our repudiating God.

We may repudiate God, but God never repudiates *us*.

Jesus promises that He will never leave us or desert us. In the barrenness of life and in the emptiness of death, He assures us: *You are never alone.*

"I will not leave you desolate . . ." Jesus promises (John 14:18). The word in the Greek New Testament is the origin for our English word *orphan*. Lonely though we may feel, Jesus states that He will not leave us orphans. Through the Spirit, He stands with us!

3

We Have Jesus—
That's Enough

One of my first jobs while I was in high school was with an outdoor advertising company that specialized in billboards. My first day on the job taught me several unforgettable lessons.

The boss drove a man named Harold and me to a billboard that had huge peeling patches of old paper. "Harold will show you how to scrape," the boss announced. "I'll be back in a couple of hours. And get that board clean. I want to see it scraped down to bare metal."

Harold handed me a scraper, then picked up another one and demonstrated how to clean the billboard by removing a few easily peeled blotches of old paper. Harold then stepped aside.

I pushed the ten-foot pole with the scraper at the end under the accumulated paper and old dried paste on the huge signboard. Soon my neck grew stiff from craning upward. The scraper seemed to grow perceptibly heavier with each stroke. I looked around for Harold.

Harold was sitting below, filing the edge of his scraper with slow, deliberate strokes. I continued working. After a long time, Harold shuffled up to the billboard platform and handed me the scraper he'd just sharpened in exchange for the one I'd been using. He climbed down again and began sharpening my scraper. Meanwhile I continued working on removing the paper.

By this time, my shoulders ached from the constant upward pushing, and a sharp pain stabbed across my back. I glanced down. I noticed Harold had finished filing the other scraper and was standing with a coffee cup in his hand, studying the highway. Later, I looked down again. This time, I saw Harold ambling slowly around the base of the billboard, leisurely picking up the chunks of paper I had scraped loose. By this time, the scraper (which weighed about as much as a large garden hoe) seemed to require superhuman effort to manipulate. My neck and shoulders tormented me.

Finally, Harold climbed up to the platform and began to give some light swipes with his scraper. Minutes later, the boss's truck chugged up to where we were working. Harold looked industrious.

"Good job, Harold!" yelled the boss.

Then I noticed that Harold had managed to position himself in an area that I had just finished scraping, and appeared to have just completed an arduous morning's work, whereas I had moved on to tackle an unfinished corner. Then the boss shouted at me. "C'mon, Bill. Put your shoulders into it!"

That day I truly learned what it is to feel unappreciated!

Since that day, I have become aware that this is a universal human feeling. Everyone I meet testifies to having these feelings at some time.

The late Vice-president Alben Barkley once told of a time he felt unappreciated. He had heard of an old constituent who had declared publicly several times that he wasn't going to vote for Barkley in the coming senatorial election. Hurt and surprised, Barkley made a trip back to the Tennessee hills to see the man.

"What's this I hear about you telling folks you're not going to vote for me?" asked the senator.

"Yep. That's right."

"Why is that?"

"You never do nuthin'," replied the old mountaineer.

Barkley, surprised, said to the man, "Why Teecee, don't you remember how I got your uncle that job on the highway department, and how I got that bridge fixed in your hollow after that flood last spring, and how I persuaded the bank to hold off on that foreclosure on your farm when you were having problems, and how I arranged for your sister's girl to go to Nashville when she got into trouble back a few years? What do you mean I don't do anything for you?"

"Yeah," drawled the old mountaineer, spitting a stream of tobacco juice. "That may be true, but what've you done for me lately?"

No matter how much you do, it seems that you will not be appreciated the way you deserve—not ever. There will be times when you will not feel adequately appreciated. You will make sacrifices and another will get the credit. You will exert yourself and no one will notice. Regardless of what your job is or how mature you are, you will get messages telling you others aren't as grateful as they should be for what you do or who you are. You identify with Martha in the story of the dinner she and her sister prepared one evening for Jesus (*see* Luke 10:38–42).

The Blame Game

Remember Martha? She doesn't feel appreciated. She sniffs to herself, "I seem to do all the work around here. Why is everything up to me? Why doesn't Mary, my sister, help? Look at her! The lady of leisure, sitting there coolly with Jesus while I have to sweat in this kitchen."

Martha handles her feelings the same way you and I do: She blames them on her sister, Mary. "If Mary would only bestir herself and help get the meal on the table, I wouldn't feel the way I do." Martha shifts the problem to someone else.

I identify with Martha. It's so comforting to blame Mary, or Harold, or your parents. Blame Mary or Harold, but blame somebody!

It's similar to the young actor who didn't feel he was appreciated. A college drama department was presenting Shakespeare's *Hamlet* at a well-known drama festival. The night before the big production, the man playing Hamlet was rushed to the hospital and his understudy, a brash young sophomore with an exaggerated idea of his acting abilities, was thrust into the lead role. Unfortunately, the sophomore stand-in proved to be disastrously inexperienced as an actor. Instead of acting the part of Hamlet in Shakespeare's magnificent tragedy, the young man proved himself to be an egotistical ham.

The audience grew increasingly restless. As the silly performance of the sophomoric replacement continued, muttering could be heard throughout the theater. The point of no return, however, was reached when the youngster mangled the moving soliloquy of Hamlet and hisses and boos and catcalls broke out from the audience. Still not comprehending that his poor acting was the cause of the dissatisfaction, and feeling that the audience wasn't appreciating him, the lad stopped in the middle of the great soliloquy, stepped to the front of the stage, and announced innocently to the house, "Hey, look, I didn't write this stuff!"

The real problem when I feel unappreciated is not my sister, Mary, or anyone else. The real problem is *me!*

I need to sit at Jesus' feet. I am distracted with much serving. I'm agitated inwardly and outwardly. I am anxious and troubled about many things. When I am not close to God, I cannot stand myself, I cannot get along with others, and I cannot cope with life. I feel no one appreciates me.

One of the problems in our culture is that we are too work oriented. If a person is not busy, he or she is labeled lazy. We are disdainful of the person who is not a sweaty bustler and striver. Overseas visitors admire our activist mentality but also point out that it leaves no time or place for quiet and prayer.

Is this the way it is in your life? Are you so much the Martha that you have angry feelings toward others, feeling you're never appreciated?

Who's in Charge Here?

The Martha in me wants to dominate, to run things, to be in charge, to direct everything for my convenience. When others don't do as I want, I feel I'm not appreciated.

There once was a young minister who fretted because his church officers didn't make calls as he told them to. He complained that the ushers didn't pass out the bulletins and take up the offering as they had been instructed. He grew exasperated at the altar guild for not arranging the flowers the way he had asked them. The choir didn't sing as he had commanded. The people at the prayer meeting didn't pray the way they were supposed to pray. One day the minister blew up in front of one of the church leaders—a quiet, older woman. After the minister finished his recitation of complaints, the woman remained silent. Finally, she replied.

"Son," this saintly woman said gently, "I hope someday

you'll learn that God has called you to be in sales, not in management."

That young minister had to learn that lesson. So did Martha. So does this older minister! And so do you! Jesus Christ must manage, not we. *He* must be in control.

Phillips Brooks, the spellbinding preacher of Boston and author of such favorite church songs as "O Little Town of Bethlehem," started out to be a schoolteacher. He accepted a position as a Latin instructor in a boys' school near Boston. In spite of Brooks' dedication and proficiency, he was unappreciated. His students treated him disrespectfully. Brooks wrote to a friend, "They [his pupils] are the most disagreeable set of creatures without exception that I have ever met. . . . I really am ashamed of it, but I am tired, cross and almost dead, so good night."

Not long afterward, the school dismissed him from his teaching position. Adding to the sense of not being appreciated was the cutting remark of the headmaster who told Brooks that it was his observation that the person who failed at teaching failed in everything else.

Smarting under the lashes of ingratitude, Phillips Brooks wrote, "I don't know what will become of me, and I don't care much. I shall not study a profession. I wish I were fifteen years old again. Somehow, I don't seem in the way to come to much now." Embittered by the lack of appreciation at the school, Brooks even refused to see his closest friends.

Fortunately for both Phillips Brooks and the Christian church, a miracle of healing occurred. The living Lord transformed this hurt and angry schoolteacher into the heroic and effective evangelist of Copley Square. Jesus Christ saved Brooks from being devoured by his feelings of being unappreciated.

Ironically, more than any other person, Jesus had reason to feel unappreciated. Yet He never whined or wept because others did not appreciate Him adequately. Nor did He blame others or give way to self-pity.

Jesus is the Deliverer. He is God truly among us. Emmanuel, the earliest name for Jesus, says literally: "God *is* with us!"

Our problem is that we often believe only in the past tense. "God *was* with us. Once upon a time, a long time ago in a faraway place . . ." is what we seem to imply by the way we complain. We are frequently what someone called a "theoretical theist"—one who accepts the possibility of God's being among us in biblical times, but only in theory with us now. We cannot always make that leap between the New Testament ways and modern times.

God through Jesus Christ has been among us, is among us, and will be among us. Our complaints reveal our forgetfulness of His goodness and nearness. Our grumbling shows our failure to respond to His presence with us in the wilderness of life.

Take Up Your Cross

Why bother helping others when so little gratitude is shown? Why pour out your life in service when you never get thanked? Why waste your efforts in living a Christian life when no one seems to appreciate them? Why persist in sacrificing for others when you're unappreciated?

This is God's problem with each of us! He was never appreciated, yet at the cross we see that He "wasted" his life for us. He bothered with us in spite of not being appreciated.

Therefore, we persist in sacrificing. We may never be thanked, and we will seldom enjoy testimonial banquets or ticker-tape parades, but we do not need accolades and framed certificates of appreciation. We have Jesus Christ. Having a relationship with Him, we find we do not need the plaudits and prizes our culture gives. We have Jesus Christ; we have enough.

When we accept a cross and give ourselves to others without concern for thanks, the Lord seems to pull back the curtains of heaven for a brief moment and provide us a glimmer of Presence! And that suffices. We have these brief glimpses of glory when we "waste" our lives sacrificing for others. He whispers afresh, "Because I live, you shall live also when you take up your cross!"

A couple of years ago, we joined a couple in our congregation in celebrating their fortieth wedding anniversary. It was a pleasant evening, filled with laughter and reminiscing.

The most vivid memory this couple cherished was the witness of the minister who had married them. It seems that the night before he married them, this man received word that his only son had been killed in action. The couple told him that they would find another minister to perform the wedding ceremony. In spite of the minister's personal grief, he insisted on joining the young couple the following day for their marriage. He sacrificed his own desire to retreat into tears and loneliness and carried out his responsibilities. He never realized the impact he made on that bride and groom by standing with them in their hour of joy despite his pain. They confessed that they never told him how much they appreciated what he did, but they acknowledged that his example made them determine to be active in the church throughout their married life, which they have done.

Who knows who may be affected by your throwing away your life for others? Who knows what child, what enemy, what indifferent man or woman will be touched with a glimpse of the cross through your sacrifice?

The early Christians used to speak of red martyrdom and white martyrdom, red being those who literally had life snatched from them, like Stephen, and white being the apparently less heroic giving of one's life without being executed for the faith. Most of us are called to white martyrdom and the daily dying of little deaths. But what effects our sacrifices have! God surprises us unexpectedly with what He does with our witness. What seems to be a waste according to the world will be a witness for God! In God's economy, no sacrifice for Christ is ever a waste!

4

He Is Going
Before Us to Galilee

A few years ago, a New York bus driver briefly became a folk hero. Weary of the job of steering his bus around the same route dozens of times each day, one afternoon he turned to his passengers and told them they'd have to get off. Then he headed his bus out of the city. The police finally caught up with him and the bus in Florida. His superiors stated that they'd fired the driver. Public sympathy for the driver was so great, however, that they had to relent and give him his old job back. It seemed everyone could identify with the bus driver's feelings about his job.

Life is a dreary, routine matter for many people. When a

group of British astronomers and astrophysicists recently issued fake passports and tickets to the planet Mars to some of
their fellow scientists, they weren't prepared for the response. The newspapers picked up the joke, and suddenly
hundreds of people wrote to the astronomers, many sending
money, expressing readiness to leave the humdrum of this
planet for life on Mars.

One psychiatrist calls the sense of boredom arising from
everyday routine "Chronic Circular Suburbanitis." Because
his patients experience the same get-up time, the same
breakfast, the same commute to the job, the same work each
day with the same people, the same routine each evening, he
says their death certificates should actually read "Died of
boredom."

The dreary, daily grind takes its toll. Metallurgists point
out that what wears out steel high-tension wires is not the
great gusts of wind but the constant vibration that reduces
the tensile strength by wearing down the molecules. People
are also casualties of routine.

In the ancient world, the sense of *ennui* was so pervasive
that tombs were inscribed merely with the letters *N F F N S
N C* as an epitaph. The letters *N F F N S N C* stood for the
Latin words *Non Fui, Fui, Non Sum, Non Curo,* and mean "I
was not, I was, I am not, I care not." This phrase was so common in the early days of the Roman empire that it was not
necessary to reproduce the words on tombs; the first letter of
each word would do. Everyone knew, and most believed
the cynical message they convey. The words on those Roman tombs could well be the motto for many bored people
today.

Boredom seems to afflict people in every social and economic strata. Here is Colonel "Buzz" Aldrin, famed astro-
naut. After the moon walk, he felt he had nowhere to go but
down. He was acclaimed as a success, but he said, "I was an
inert Ping-Pong ball, batted about by the whims and motiva-

tions of others. I was suffering from what the poets called 'the melancholy of all things done.' "

A woman may be attractive and intelligent, but tired of the drab routine of wiping children's noses, never getting caught up with the ironing, trying to make conversation with a tired husband with nothing much to talk about.

A retiree resents the euphemisms "senior citizen" and "golden age." She resists being pushed into the childish role of attending nursery school for the old folks through quilting classes and bridge tournaments three mornings a week. But being a surplus human through retirement is boring, she acknowledges. She remembers that having a job is the certificate of worth and usefulness in our society. She would agree with Herbert Hoover's words on his eighty-second birthday, when he said that a person retiring from work "shrivels up into a nuisance to all mankind."

Jimmy Porter, a character in John Osborne's play "Look Back in Anger," has a line revealing the secret thoughts of many young people today: "Nobody thinks. Nobody cares. There aren't any good, brave causes left. If the big bang does come, and we all get killed off, it'll be just for the brave new nothing-very-much, thank you." Not surprisingly, boredom is given as a leading cause of teenage alcohol and drug abuse.

The routine of the job is one of the leading sources of boredom for countless others. Dostoevski has written, "There is one punishment so terrible that even hardened criminals tremble at the prospect, and that is simply this: to take a man's life-work and render it meaningless."

According to a study by the University of Michigan's Survey Research Center not long ago, over 27 percent of the workers in the United States are overqualified for their jobs. The survey revealed that this is especially true for recent college graduates. Boredom and routine quickly come to anyone who is overqualified. Ask the person with a liberal arts degree who is driving a taxi.

God persists in introducing Himself to people in the midst

of the routine and boring parts of life. The Lord disclosed Himself to Moses as Moses was tending sheep. God presented Himself to Gideon while Gideon was trampling grapes. The Eternal made Himself known to David while the shepherd boy was looking after the flock. God intruded into Elisha's life while Elisha was plowing. In the person of Jesus, He called Peter and Andrew, James and John as they were mending their nets. He summoned Matthew as he was sitting at his desk in the tax office. The Lord seems to have a preference for approaching people in the midst of the daily grind.

Even the spiritual highs that took place during the time Jesus was on earth were always followed by reminders that those who experienced these mountaintop moments were to return to the everyday routine. God apparently doesn't intend to have us exist in a perpetual spiritual jag. The shepherds visit the manger, but are immediately sent back to the boredom of the dark hillside with their sheep. Peter, James and John ascend the Mount of Transfiguration with Jesus, but are brought back to the commonplace world of distraught fathers and sick kids. The disciples and the risen Lord are told to return to the boring old grind of Galilee.

"Okay," you are probably saying, "so maybe the Lord affected some folks like those disciples in their everyday routine. But not me! Not in my dull, boring world."

You may be a religious *nimby*, the term applied to obstructionists and protesters shouting, "Not in my back yard!" whenever any unwanted intrusion comes into their community. You may dismiss any promises of God coming into your daily routine with a cynical *nimby* attitude: "God could not or would not come into my back yard."

Actually, what is so boring to you may not be your job or your surroundings or the people around you. It may be you!

Boredom is within ourselves. "Someone's boring me. . . . I think it's me," Dylan Thomas lamented.

An ancient fable speaks of the king who called his prime minister in and stated, "I have been looking out the window for the past few days and observe that everyone seems so bored and everything looks so boring."

"Begging your pardon, your majesty," replied the prime minister, "but that it is not a window. It is a mirror!"

A New Perspective

If we see only our own images, we will be bored. But Jesus Christ brings us a new perspective.

A few years ago, Bell Laboratories came up with a fascinating invention. It was a box slightly smaller than an ordinary breadbox. When a certain button was pushed, machinery started inside. The lid of the box would quietly open, then a hand would come up and slowly reach over the side of the box and shut off the mechanism. The hand would then go back into the box and the lid would close. The silly but interesting device had no useful purpose; it was merely a toy that turned itself off. Some people seem to be like that. They never let themselves find any useful purpose in life; they merely exist to turn themselves off.

Through Jesus Christ, however, God plans for you to be helpful and productive. Put the Lord first and discover for yourself that you are meant to be more than a worthless machine closing the lid on life.

". . . Behold, I make all things new . . ." the risen One announces (Revelation 21:5). *All* things—including everyday life! For the believer, every day is God's new gift, a source of wonder and of joy. The man or woman who knows the risen Lord knows that something of importance is occurring every moment! God brings new life to our world, introducing new directions for history. God persists in rearranging events to meet His ends.

History has direction . . . our lives have purpose . . . human existence has a destiny. And praise God that you and I are part of the story of the new heaven and new earth and the new Jerusalem the Lord promises!

"I make all things new"—including your life, my friend!

This living Jesus Christ can still perform miracles, including raising you from the torpor of being bored to death. Expect great things from Him! Ask great things from Him! Then do great things for Him!

The motto of the Spanish royal coat of arms used to be *Ne Plus Ultra* ("There's no more beyond here") because Spaniards thought they were perched on the farthest point of the world, beyond which there was nothing. When Columbus returned from his famous voyage the king and queen of Spain, Ferdinand and Isabella, learned that there was more beyond. Suddenly their coat of arms seemed inappropriate. Someone quickly amended it by dropping the Latin word *Ne* so that the inscription read *Plus Ultra* ("There is more beyond").

"No more beyond here" seemed to be the final word for everything at Calvary, until God interrupted this cycle and demonstrated He is even in control of death. *Plus Ultra!* There is more beyond! "Behold, I make all things new!"

He also makes all things new in your life. *All* things new, even though you may think the last chapter has been written or the last trick played or the last play called.

A fourteen-year-old girl received a diary for her birthday. Her first entry read: "Got a diary from Grandma, but it's too late because everything has happened already."

Contrast that autobiographical note with Paul's, "If any one is in Christ, he is a new creation . . ." (2 Corinthians 5:17). The risen Lord, as the apostle knew, turns the dull prose of life into the lilting poetry of life as an adventure.

To Galilee

You may think that the New Testament is something like a time machine taking us back to the first century and showing us the face of a great teacher who was put to death on a cross. You may even try to think that on Christmas or Easter, Jesus may seem more alive than dead. Mark's Gospel account will not let you think that, when you ponder its ending.

However, it's a strange ending. Mark describes the crucifixion. He gives the details of the desolation and agony of Jesus on the cross. He tells us that Jesus died. Mark states that Jesus' body was taken by Joseph of Arimathea and laid in a rock tomb, and that at least two women watched and noted the place. Then Mark informs us that on the Jewish sabbath, the Saturday, everyone rested.

Before sunup on Sunday, two women came to put aromatic ointment around the shrouded corpse, worrying how they'd manage to heave the heavy wheellike stone away from the tomb opening. He relates that they were surprised: The tomb was empty.

A young man sitting there tells them, "Do not be amazed; you seek Jesus of Nazareth, who was crucified. He has risen, he is not here; see the place where they laid him. But go, tell his disciples and Peter that he is going before you to Galilee; there you will see him, as he told you" (Mark 16:6, 7).

Mark reports that the women rushed out, frightened and bewildered. He states how the women reacted, and suddenly he stops in midsentence. At the end of Mark 16:8, the final word is the little Greek word *gar*, which means "for" and is never at the end of a proper sentence, but always introduces another thought. Mark's ending is abrupt.

If you're reading in the original New Testament Greek, your reaction is, "Yes? Continue, please. Go on! What's next? Don't drop it there!"

For a while, some scholars thought that the ending of Mark had been lost or that the original scroll had become so worn at the end that it had dropped off. These scholars were saying, "Aw, come on, Mark, don't leave everything hanging like that. What's next? Keep going. Tell us more about Jesus appearing to people that first Easter."

Mark's ending is his way of saying, "Now the ball is in your court. The real record of the risen Lord comes from you! You write the rest of the sentence; you finish the chapter! Now *you* get involved!" Mark's conclusion is a good literary device that involves you and me in the Resurrection. It puts you to work. It is inductive preaching at its best. The end of Mark's Gospel report is only the beginning of Christ's work with you! Mark draws you into the story!

"No more?" you ask when you read Mark's ending, "Nothing more to be said?" Of course there's more. He is alive; but it is to be said by *you!*

"But wait a minute," you say. "All this took place about nineteen hundred plus years ago. What do you mean that Mark is involving me? What do you want me to do, play the time-machine game with Easter?"

Listen again to the message: ". . . he is going before you to Galilee; there you will see him, as he told you."

To Galilee. To the world of leaky boats and smelly nets, chilly nights and sudden storms; the world of risky fishing and uncertain markets, hard work and everyday relationships. To Galilee: the home turf; daily routine; the area where nonbelievers live.

The place you will encounter the risen living Lord is in the Monday-to-Friday world this week, when you take up discipleship in His Name. "There you will see him, as He told you!"

Don't look for dramatic disclosures and dazzling visions, but expect the presence of Jesus in your Galilee, your world of annoying customers, tiring days and sleepless nights, problem people and strenuous service for Him. "He is going before you to Galilee." Jesus is alive and at work in the world beyond the walls of your church. He claims His lordship. The announcement of the living Lord comes weekly during worship, but the *real* encounter with the risen Jesus Christ will take place as you leave to meet Him in your Galilee!

5

He Never Puts Down
The Honest Seeker

Richard Janson, eight other boys and I were seated in the high-school-boys' Sunday-school class in our tiny cubicle of a classroom. Richard and the rest of us listened patiently to the lesson on Jonah. The teacher seemed primarily concerned with establishing the point that Jonah had survived his time inside a whale and emerged none the worse. Richard found this difficult to understand. He asked a series of questions. The teacher, determined to ram across the point he held—that every word of Scripture must be taken at face value with no questions asked—tried to cow Richard into silence.

Richard, our resident brain, was undaunted. Pressing on, he firmly pointed out to the teacher that there are no whales in the Mediterranean. How could the teacher talk about not asking questions?

Testily, the teacher replied, "Richard, why do you question?" and continued with a stern lecture about never raising any questions about the faith.

I've sometimes wondered where Richard is now. I do know that many Richards have dropped out of the Church because they were told they must surrender their intellectual integrity. I suspect that there are Richards who may still be privately struggling with doubts and questions and feel guilty about having them.

I know other Richards who have tried to reach some sort of accommodation with their questions and doubts. For instance, I know a woman with questions about the wording of the Apostles' Creed. She was afraid to question what the words mean, lest she be accused of being unchristian. Therefore she simply remained silent every time the congregation repeated the creed in worship.

Perhaps you have had experiences similar to hers or Richard Janson's. Maybe you are uneasy over being told that you must not question.

Let's say it plainly: Jesus never put down the honest seeker. He never condemned the doubter. He differentiates between doubt and unbelief.

Doubt or Unbelief?

Doubt is "I *cannot* believe." Unbelief is "I *will not* believe." Doubt is looking for light; unbelief prefers the dark. Doubt is weighing the evidence; unbelief is playing with evasions. Let's look at some examples of doubt as opposed to unbelief.

A couple of years ago, a tanker slammed into the Sunshine Skyway Bridge across Tampa Bay, obliterating a quarter-

mile section of roadway and hurtling thirty-eight people in
vehicles to their deaths. A driver was more fortunate and
skidded to a stop only fourteen inches from the brink of the
gaping hole in the road, one hundred forty feet above the
choppy waters. He was quoted as saying, "I figure the Lord
was real good to the four of us." When a preacher later
quoted the driver and extolled his piety, someone asked,
"What about the thirty-eight who were crushed and
drowned? Why wasn't the Lord as good to them?" The
preacher chided the questioner, "You must not ask!"

A pastor I know had a son who joined the navy. After boot
camp, the boy was sent to San Diego for sea duty. The night
before the young man was to ship out, the pastor received a
telephone call from his son saying good-bye.

The pastor was proud of the son and pleased with the boy's
thoughtfulness. Several hours later, the pastor received another call. Immediately after leaving the telephone booth, his
son was jumped by three young hoodlums and stabbed to
death. The three assailants were high on drugs and had killed
for kicks; they had never seen the boy before. The pastor-
father of the slain sailor had been active in working for the
rights and advancement of minority groups, and the killers of
his own son were all members of a minority group. We could
well understand if that distraught father questioned, "What
is the point of anything anymore?"

This is doubt. The person asking the preacher about the
thirty-eight killed in Tampa Bay and the pastor-father of the
murdered sailor are in the doubting category. They are in the
"I *cannot* believe" school, not the "I *will not* believe!"

Jesus does not condemn *doubt*. He condemns *unbelief*.

Examples of unbelief abound in the Gospel accounts. The
scribes and Pharisees who disparaged Jesus and His claims
are examples of unbelief. After Jesus healed the paralyzed
man and assured him that his sins were forgiven, the scribes
seethed. They critically and self-righteously clucked that

only God can forgive. "Who does Jesus think He is? How does He think He can get away with this nonsense? He's upsetting our culture! Why should we allow Him to threaten all we hold sacred?"

Jesus takes in their thoughts, reading them very clearly. Jesus asks, "Why do you question . . . ?" (Mark 2:8). Jesus knows their questions are not doubt, but unbelief.

Doubt is looking for light; unbelief is relishing the darkness. Doubt is honesty; unbelief is obstinacy. Doubt is weighing the evidence; unbelief is playing with evasions. "Why do you question?" that is, "Why do you insist on arguing within yourselves?" as the Greek word *dialogizomai* states. "Why do you scorn me? Why do you belittle me?"

The unbeliever finds fault with God. Here is a handy list of scribes who may be observed today:

The Artful Dodger.   Evades commitment at all cost. Frequently well read and well informed on matters of biblical scholarship and theological discussion. Sophisticated dilettante. "Oh, no, of course I'm not a member of any congregation. Can't be bothered with associating with others. Too hypocritical." Ignores requirements of serious discipleship. Subspecies of Artful Dodgers:

> *Window Shopper.* "Trying out" different churches. Never finds one totally satisfactory. Or dabbles in many religions and practices, including astrology, transcendental meditation, various promoters on the electronic church.
> *Shoplifter.* Takes without paying for it. Wants all the benefits of the Christian life—without any sacrifice or commitment. Demands first-class religious programs for children and for himself on festive occasions such as Christmas and Easter, but will not pray, pledge or participate personally.

The Sophomore.   Not questioning the Christian faith so much as questioning his/her own misunderstanding of it.

Relishes identifying inconsistencies, real or imagined, in doctrine. Eager to show how impractical faith or Christian service is. Takes the *Wall Street Journal*'s sometimes erroneous interpretations of the Gospel as an authority over the New Testament. Subspecies of Sophomores:

Showboat. Professional scoffer and faultfinder with the faith, the Church and its attempts to minister in Christ's name. Loves to entertain an audience at parties with clever dialectic, interesting anecdotes and provocative arguments about weaknesses and failures of Christians and Christianity.

Sloganeer. Thinks in terms of phrases on bumper stickers. Delights in repeating clichés such as, "All religion's the same"; "Everyone's going to the same place, anyhow"; "If only everyone would live by the Golden Rule" (usually everybody else except themselves); "Charity begins at home"; "What's mine is mine, and I have a God-given right to keep it"; "We're God's chosen people here, and I don't care what happens to the rest"; "Nobody's ever had to look after me. If only 'they' would get jobs or go back to where 'they' came from, everything would be better"; "God helps them who help themselves."

Jesus has little to say to the Artful Dodgers and the Sophomores. He knows they are practicing unbelief and not expressing honest doubts.

The Answer to Doubt

There are times in everyone's life when things go badly and doubts arise. You will have such moments. It's not that you have sunk into atheism. It's just that it is hard to believe, especially when life seems to tumble in. It is not that you disbelieve; it's simply hard to believe!

Most of us carry the notion that we are evil and wrong to have any doubts like these. We remember our Sunday-school days as children (the last time most of us had any instruction in the Christian faith), when some lovable but misinformed old saint taught our classes. Whenever any little skeptic raised a question that she did not have a stock answer for, she would look disapprovingly and tell us, "Now, now, we must not question God."

Now ten, twenty, or thirty years later, you have doubts. You are uneasy. Suffering has smelted out many of the glib assumptions you had toward life and toward God. But you feel guilty. You were told that it is wrong to doubt. To think that it is a sin to have doubts is mistake number one in dealing with doubt.

Mistake number two is to think that all you need are some smart, sensible answers to your questions.

A man hanging on a cross asked the same question in His dying moments. Gasping for breath, fighting for life, Jesus went through dark moments of doubt: "My God, my God, why hast Thou forsaken me?"

We shy away from these words from the cross. We try to tamper with them. We do not like to admit that Jesus doubted. We try to take the horror out of this phrase, remove the loneliness by substituting what we *think* Jesus really meant. Yet there it stands. In spite of our efforts to tailor it to fit our schemes, the phrase stands bleak and stark as a cliff. Why would Jesus have said these words—unless He meant them?

At the cross, our Savior doubted. In the sweaty, bloody agony and loneliness of the crucifixion, He, too, asked "Why?" Pain, injustice, loneliness and death seemed to be running the universe. Defeat and evil seemed to have the last word. Everything seemed to be the opposite from what it was supposed to be. He asked that question once and for all. He asked it for every person, for you and me. We do not need to ask that question ever again.

We know now that God does not slap us down for impertinence when we ask questions in our times of doubt. He does not tell us to shut up and sit down. We know that God does not hand us an answer book. He does not invite us into His office for a chat on how things are run at headquarters.

God does neither. In the cross and Resurrection, our God comes to us, stands with us. He does not forsake or forget us. He draws near and gives us Himself.

So you're a doubter as a result of suffering. Your question has already been asked. Your doubts have already been put into words. God already knows them—more clearly than you know them yourself. There is no need to ask. God Himself is with us!

When I was a small boy, I was taken to the circus. Somehow, I got separated from my parents and wandered around lost for two hours. I tried to find my folks, but to no avail. Then I thought I'd return to the car, but I couldn't locate it. Then I thought I would walk home, but after walking a few blocks, I knew I was hopelessly lost and tried to make my way back to the circus grounds. To a very small child, this is an experience of real suffering.

Meanwhile, some doubts began to creep into my mind. Maybe my parents did not love me anymore. Maybe they were trying to get rid of me. What would I do? Who would feed me? Where would I go? Why didn't they come? *Where were they?*

These were dark moments of doubt for a four-year-old. Unbeknownst to me, my father was seeking, searching, waiting. He would never have slept until he located his little boy. He spared no effort in finding that little lost son. He finally found that boy, much to my relief.

So in our doubts, God is with us and is concerned. We doubt, but we really do not need to cry "Why?" anymore. Our God has gotten through to us in the living, risen Jesus Christ. In our wandering, in our loneliness, in our heartache, in our pain, we doubt.

But we have a waiting Father—a seeking, searching Father who can never forsake you, who will never forget you. You doubt Him, perhaps, but He is trustworthy! He is faithful!

God Accepts the Doubter

The Apostle Thomas was the original "man from Missouri," the person who asked questions. He was also a man hit hard by the crucifixion of Jesus. He knew the ghastly details of a man dying on the cross. He also knew how unjust this atrocity was.

It was an upside-down world when such things went on. It was a life that blew aside all the simple, romantic answers. Thomas was let down, cynical, questioning.

The other disciples talked about Jesus Christ alive again. Thomas, however, was not swept off his feet by this report. He would not let himself grow excited about it. He was realistic. He wanted things he could see and feel. Thomas was honest: "Jesus was dead; it is impossible for dead men to rise up."

When the others pressed him, Thomas was blunt. Until he personally poked his fingers into the nail holes in Jesus' palms, he did not want to listen. But nothing happened. A day passed, then a week. Still no sign, no proof. "No sign, no God," Thomas was probably thinking. He doubted.

But the risen Lord stood by Thomas. He accepted the doubter.

Thomas discovered that doubt gives way to faith not by the removal of intellectual difficulties or by proofs through tests but by the presence of the Lord. Thomas understood that Jesus was with him. Thomas learned that God wanted to renew fellowship with him through the risen Lord.

Perhaps you have put up some tests for God. Or maybe you have demanded some sign from the Lord. You insist on some proof for faith. "If God gets me out of this jam, I'll believe Him," you say. You sound like a scheming boss, setting up clever little tests to make sure a questionable employee is on the job. You check up on God.

If you have been "trying" God out, if you've been considering a "deal" with God, if you've been checking Him out, forget it! This has all been done once and for all time. It's been done for you and for all people. In coming to Thomas, God in Christ brushed aside all your tests.

One summer while I was still in seminary, I worked as a laborer in a mining camp in Alaska. One of the men in my gang was a young veteran who had deep doubts about God. Henry had survived the mud, heat, rain and bullets of the South Pacific. He had watched his closest buddies chewed apart with debilitating disease and sieved by snipers' bullets.

Where was God, Henry wanted to know. How could God allow such senseless waste of good men's lives in their best years? How could there be any reason behind the universe in the midst of such chaos and stupidity? Henry said he wanted to believe, but he would have to have some answers and proofs first. Meanwhile he had dropped out of Harvard and was bumming his way from job to job without any purpose or goal.

We argued and discussed. As a smart aleck young theological student, I had read the books. I had all the answers. I proudly racked up points for the Lord's side by doing battle with this young infidel. I had a comeback for everything that Henry said. I could refute every doubt. I could answer logically and sensibly (so I thought!) every deep, puzzling question Henry brought up.

Henry and I both thought that all he needed was answers. We assumed that if he knew the right answers to his questions, Henry would be a Christian. And so we played our little question and answer game.

Henry, however, did not really need answers. Henry did not really *want* answers. Henry really needed a *friend*.

Feel the Tug

A couple of summers ago at Cape Cod, we were flying a kite on the beach on an overcast day. The kite was soaring high in the sky. Suddenly, a heavy fog swept in, as sometimes happens in New England. The mists obscured the kite. One of our young grandsons looked up in dismay. He could not see his kite. His little face clouded in perplexity. Where was his kite? It was up there still, his daddy explained. But how did daddy know? Daddy had a simple answer: "Here," he said. "I can feel the tug!"

You have felt the tug of the reality of the Spirit more than you realize. The very fact that you are reading this book at this time is evidence of the tug of the Spirit in your life this day! The fact that you decided at one point to commit your life to Jesus Christ is the result of the tug. The fact that you feel the need to pray to say thank you, or to ask for help, or to want forgiveness is due to the tug of the Spirit.

You do not possess the Spirit—the Spirit possesses you! You do not control the Spirit; the Spirit controls you. You may think you hold the Spirit, but actually the Spirit clutches you. He tugs!

God is not a theorem to be proved. God is not an object to be studied. God will be known only by an adventure of friendship.

Faith is not a matter of proofs. Faith is a matter of trust. There is no substitute for trust. No one can manufacture faith. No one can prove God. The Bible assumes faith, giving no proofs for His existence. You must start in your Christian pilgrimage by *assuming* that you already have faith.

The only analogy that makes sense in this matter of faith is the analogy of two people getting married. When you marry, you have no proof of the fidelity of the other. You must rely completely on the word of the other person that he or she will remain faithful. You realize, too, that you really do not

know the other that well. In many ways, you are still somewhat strangers to each other.

In a sense, this is all very risky. You know the statistics of
marriages breaking up, and they make you somewhat shaky
inside: You have no certainty that this will not happen to
you.

Your marriage must be a matter of trust. You simply will
have no proofs—you must depend upon the word of your
partner. In spite of your secret doubts and inner skepticism,
you finally commit yourself. You bet your life on the word of
the other person.

So it is with God. You have no proofs of His presence or
His goodness. You have only His word that He remains faithful. Ultimately, you must take Him at His word.

You can trust God. You can put your confidence in Him,
even though you may have your intellectual problems, un-
answered questions and recurring doubts. In Jesus Christ,
God gives you His word that He remains faithful. You have
the personal pledge of the personal God.

There once was a family whose home caught fire in the
middle of the night. The parents woke their children and
quickly led them out. The five-year-old, however, slipped
away and ran back upstairs. It wasn't until they were outside
that they saw him in a second-story window surrounded by
smoke. The boy's father yelled, "Jump! I'll catch you!"

"But, Daddy," the child protested, "I can't see you."

The father cried, "But I can see you, and that's all that
matters. *Jump!*"

We may say that we cannot see God. But God can see us.
This we know through Jesus Christ. In the person of Jesus,
God makes Himself known as one who sees and cares and
saves.

Make your leap of faith!

6

On the Side of
The Ultimate Victor

In the ancient city of Beijing (formerly known as Peking), the magnificent Forbidden City stands as a monument to China's rich heritage. A beautiful shrine with the name The Pavilion of Preserved Peace is found at the center of the Forbidden City.

Two tourists were discussing the lovely shrine with its intriguing name. "I wish life could be a perpetual pavilion of preserved peace for me," commented the first.

Recognizing the desire to be free of conflict and yet knowing that life is never free of strife, the second visitor replied, "Yes, and that's why it's in the Forbidden City!"

We live in the midst of conflict every day. In fact, the seeds of discord between people are present in every relationship. Each time we encounter another, we have the potential for strife. We joke about the propensity for conflict among some of us. For example, Presbyterians laugh at the old story of the two Scots shipwrecked on a desert island who promptly started the First Presbyterian Church *and* the Second Presbyterian Church. Conflict is present in every scene in every society. There is no pavilion of preserved peace anywhere.

Conflict is particularly part of your workday world. "I like going to church on Sunday and being inspired by the message," a person in sales stated gloomily, "but on Monday I have to put on the brass knuckles."

Dan W. Dodson, expert on conflict resolution and author of many articles and books on managing conflict in organizations, is frequently invited to act as a consultant where tensions exist in schools. Dodson insists that there will be conflict in the best run operation. In *Power Conflict and Community Organizations* he writes:

> When I go into a school and the principal tells me "We have no problems," I know one of three things is wrong. First—he is lying—which is most often the case. Second he is not perceptive enough to know a problem when he sees it. This is sometimes the case. Or third he is so authoritarian he does not allow freedom enough for problems to come to the surface. Our problem is to deal with conflict in such manner that it does not become stultifying and destructive. A case could be made that these points of tension and conflict are the cutting edges in a free society.

Lamentably, conflicts can escalate. Frequently the original causes of conflict are obscured and the conflict takes on a life of its own. Unchecked, conflict can be destructive. In spite of the soothsayers who try to assure everybody that conflict can be healthy, conflict can also be very unhealthy. Lebanon and

Northern Ireland are case histories of conflict getting out of hand.

The world's way of resolving conflict is force. Two small children are playing in the same sandbox when each wants to dig in the same place. Conflict! Protests lead to shrieks. Shrieks give way to blows. A miniature Beirut or Belfast erupts in your backyard.

Dr. Eugene Sharpe, a professor at Harvard, has written a three-volume study on the subject of conflict. In this monumental work, he comes up with 193 ways of resolving conflict. Significantly, only one of those ways involves war or force!

The secret is to deal with conflict in ways that don't destroy the other person or yourself.

Christians Experience Conflict

Let's start by acknowledging that even Christians do not always agree. We must not kid ourselves: We Christians are people, and people are sometimes stupid, stubborn, selfish and silly. In short, we are sinful. All of which means that in spite of our claims of being Christ's, we will not always see eye-to-eye with one another. We will disagree. We will be in conflict. Whether in a home or a congregation or denomination or wherever, we will sometimes clash.

For example, here are some of the sources of disagreement in a typical American Protestant congregation:

• whether all our funds should be spent for ourselves locally and none for others overseas, or some shared with those in other lands

• whether children should sit through an entire worship service or be excused after the hymn before the sermon

• whether efforts should be made to share more with Roman Catholics or whether cooperation will be capitulation

• whether all the church programs should be focused on

spiritual matters or some should be also directed to forms of
social witness (spirituality or service)

• whether working for nuclear freeze is being naive, unpa-
triotic and playing into Communist plans, or carrying out
Christ's call of being peacemakers.

• whether real wine or unfermented grape juice should be
served at Holy Communion.

The earliest Christians also disagreed. In fact, they had lots
of controversy and conflict in the Church in the early days.
Read Acts 15 and some of Paul's letters from that period.

The Jews were used to circumcision. It was part of their
history and heritage. After all, it was the seal of the ancient
covenant with Abraham, and was as important to every Jew
as baptism is to us. The Jews who embraced Jesus as Messiah
and Savior kept circumcision, since the custom had meaning
and importance to them.

Then non-Jews began to become Christians. Some Jewish
Christians insisted that the newcomers be circumcised as
well as baptized. Other Jewish Christians didn't say too much
as long as there were only a few Gentile converts. But when
the influx of non-Jews into the Church started, it wasn't the
same. The Church's complexion began to change from being
an extension of the temple and synagogue to a movement
made up largely of non-Jews.

The hot sparks of controversy came close to bursting into
destructive flames of conflict. Acts 15 and Galatians 1 and 2
provide us with accounts of how the early Christians resolved
this potentially dangerous controversy. These accounts give
us helpful guidelines when we disagree, whether in marriage
or in church or wherever.

Centering on the Gospel

The first step is to sort out what issues are major and what
are minor, what is fundamental to the faith and what is not.

This is an effort to distinguish among truth, trivia, and tradition, remembering that the three often become tangled and intertwined.

Lloyd George, the fiery Welshman who served as England's prime minister during World War I, was once asked about his religious affiliation. George stated that he was a member of a very small Welsh Baptist sect that had split off from another tiny group because of an intense fight over wording. When asked what the wording was, George replied that one group insisted a person was baptized *into* the Holy Ghost and the other emphasized that one was baptized *of* the Holy Ghost. The interviewer inquired which group the prime minister belonged to. Lloyd George pondered a long minute, then acknowledged that he couldn't remember whether his was the group that demanded adherents be baptized *into* the Holy Ghost or *of*, but added: "But, by God, I'd die for my beliefs and my church!"

Sometimes we need to be brought up short and made to consider whether we are being faithful or merely being fussy in some of our ideas.

Friends of mine in prisoner-of-war camps preserved their Christian fellowship by focusing on the Gospel. The Chinese underground church had to learn to avoid becoming embroiled in controversy over the wrong things. In the case of the early Church in the Acts 15 account, conflict was resolved when all leaders recognized that circumcision was not required for salvation; trust in the Good News was the essential requisite.

Sensitivity to Others

Acts 15 notes that both parties in disagreement "listened." Listening is hard, especially when both parties must try to avoid both squelching and surrendering. It's hard to maintain the balance between silencing the other on one hand and remaining silent yourself. Listening means not resorting to slurs, sneers or smears. Listening means caring. Listening calls for putting the best interpretation on others.

Behind their sensitivity to one another was their sense of oneness, in spite of differences. They "gathered together to consider"; they "welcomed" each other. They referred to each other as "Brethren." All of these terms in Acts 15 indicate a regard for the other as a person, not an adversary.

A few years ago, two elders in the First Presbyterian Church of Ferguson, Missouri, were known to have sharply contrasting ideas about the church's involvement in social issues. They frequently spoke on opposite sides. Some thought their conflicting notions would bring conflict or division in their church. These two men, on their own initiative, mailed a letter to all their fellow members. It read in part:

> This is a letter from two members of Session who have different views of what the church should do about social action. We are aware that our congregation, like many others across the country, exists in a state of tension—tension induced by what the church should or should not be doing in the world. Both of us know that on some issues, we are diametrically opposed. Yet, if you come to the 11 o'clock service, much of the time you will see us sitting in adjacent pews. At Communion Services, you will see us sit side by side and serve communion together. We have served on the same church board for several years. You see, we know that our unity in Christ is greater than the differences we have with each other's thoughts about which direction the church should take. By this letter, we wish to witness to that unity. . . .
>
> (Signed) I. T. Thompson and J. T. Kress.

Submission to Christ

Disagreements between Christians must be faced in light of the fact that each of us ultimately must submit to the will of Christ.

It is not always easy to know when to make concessions or

when to stand firm, when to abandon a position and when to cherish a tradition. Disagreements between persons who are Christian, however, are always in the light of mutual submission to Christ. This means accepting the other's idiosyncracies and weaknesses, quirks and hang-ups. It always means accepting limits and making sacrifices for the sake of others because of your submission to Christ.

For example, I know a couple who choose to put Christ in the light of their freedom to use alcohol. This couple knows they are free to drink or not to drink, both realizing they are not bound by rules and that the Gospel is not legalism. Furthermore, they are not of the opinion that they are better than others because they do not drink, nor do they imagine that they are saved by being teetotalers. Rather, out of respect for their alcoholic friends, a concern for their children, and a witness to youth that chemical crutches are not indispensable for happiness or success, this couple endures the jibes and pressures of not accepting or serving drinks.

The New Testament Christians would have understood this. Do you?

Sometimes in our zeal we find ourselves taking others to task for disagreeing with our views, thinking we are sent to set right the views of others. One such person in the nineteenth century was an eccentric Scottish clergyman named Edward Irving. Irving emphasized his own peculiar views on the Second Coming and left the Church of Scotland to start a sect named the Catholic Apostolic Community. Irving's associates in the Church found him increasingly difficult to converse with as he veered further into questionable ideas and expounded them so dogmatically. His onetime friend, essayist-minister Thomas Carlyle, remarked about Irving, "He was a sent man, but he went further than he was supposed to go!"

It is all right to be aware that we are "sent," but we must not go further than we are supposed to go!

Paul, comprehending that those who know Christ's acceptance respond by submitting themselves to His will, writes, "For in Christ Jesus neither circumcision nor uncircumcision is of any avail, but faith working through love" (Galatians 5:6).

Faith working through love! That is centering on the Gospel, sensitivity to others and submission to Christ! And that's how Christians disagree without denying Christ or denying conflict.

But what about those occasions where in spite of all this, you still find yourself in conflict?

The Ultimate Victor

Edward Jenner, a clergyman's son, discovered a way to prevent deadly smallpox. Jenner had seen too many people carried off by the dread disease, and he prayed and experimented to find a way of averting the scourge. His efforts, however, embroiled him in conflict with people who objected furiously. Smallpox, they shrilled, was God's punishment for sin, and Jenner was interfering with the Almighty's powers.

Look at Elijah, who found himself in conflict with King Ahab and with Ahab's religious yes-men. Read the account of the showdown between God's prophet and the prophets of Baal and Asherah in 1 Kings 18, the classic conflict between the real God and false gods. The king denounced Elijah as a "troublemaker" (see 1 Kings 18:17, 18), further sharpening the conflict. In reality, Ahab, not Elijah, was the troublemaker, and in refusing to heed God's plans, he brought trouble on himself and his nation.⁴

In times of conflict you may feel outnumbered as one of God's people. Elijah thought he was a helpless minority of one, hated, hounded and hurt. Even the feistiest of prophets have their low moments. In your times of conflict, you may also think you are fighting impossible odds. Faith, you will quickly learn, is no ticket to ease and success in life. With

God, however, you need not whimper. You are always on the side of the ultimate Victor.

Jesus lived with conflict on a daily basis during His career. We forget that He was subjected to nasty confrontations, death threats, deep-set resistance, harsh denunciations, severe criticism, intransigent opinions, and finally imprisonment, torture and a brutal form of execution.

Jesus remained true to His calling. The cross should be the symbol of defeat through conflict; instead, in light of the Resurrection, we see Jesus' death in the face of conflict as God's plan and God's power for us. We know that in the midst of conflict, when we remain true to our calling as Christ's in the world, we will have to suffer. But we also know we shall prevail.

A young couple named Jennifer and Doug discovered this for themselves. Their arguments seemed to grow harsher and their disagreements seemed to get deeper. Jennifer began praying, understanding that she and Doug were meant to keep their marriage vows, even if she wasn't sure how. She continued to pray for strength and guidance and received help from a counselor. She discovered traits in herself that marred the relationship.

One evening, her husband seemed unusually irritable, almost spoiling for a fight. He finally found an excuse to start a severe tongue lashing. He carried on for several minutes, belittling and criticizing her. This time, Jennifer did not answer back in a counterattack. Praying for strength, she quietly walked up to him, took his hands, and with tears streaming down her face said, "Doug, I love you still."

The young husband tightened for a moment, then broke down. "I'm sorry, Jennifer, for what I've been doing. I guess you should have married a better man."

Jennifer answered softly, "I did."

She remembered the man Doug was and could be, and continued to see possibilities in her man.

You say, "God continues to have ideas and dreams and plans involving me?" Ah, but with God, nothing is impossible. The story of your life, as well as the story of the Bible, is a tale of God wanting to use you to do the impossible with Him.

Likewise for our world! "How can this be?" we ask. "How can we believe this claim that God continues to promise that His realm will prevail? How can we take seriously the announcement that the Prince of Peace has come, in the face of daily death tallies in Lebanon and Central America? Mercy and reconciliation will prevail? Justice will be carried out? Harmony and *shalom* will rule? When?"

"For with God nothing will be impossible!" God has introduced His rule throughout the entire cosmos through Jesus!

An American admiral once had a small card printed and circulated among his workers and subordinates. In gray type on the card was a background message, "It Can't Be Done." But in bold block letters across this message was the phrase, "But Here It Is!"

In the midst of the conflict you must endure, culture and community may say to you that your efforts for peace and justice can't prevail. With Jesus Christ, you know otherwise. With Him, you are God's "But Here It Is!"

7

Going Through Temptation With Jesus at Our Side

A few years ago, a little congregation in Ohio was persuaded by its pastor to escape temptation and testing once and for all. They agreed to bring all bikinis, television sets, copies of liberal publications and hard-rock records to the church parking lot and burn them in a bonfire. When the local police and fire departments pointed out that there was an ordinance barring open trash burning, the church folks agreed to change their plans and have a garbage truck arrive on the appointed Saturday. Presumably, the people in that suburb have not been bothered with testing or temptation since that time.

The problem, of course, is not external. It's internal. As Pogo put it so beautifully, "We have met the enemy and he is us."

Furthermore, we will never be free of temptation and testing. One of our peculiar delusions as Christians is that we can lift ourselves to a high enough pinnacle of spirituality to be free from the tugs of temptation and testing.

A young girl was picked up for shoplifting. Everyone in the school knew about it, although nothing was printed in the newspaper. Then the girl started attending a church and went through a great conversion experience. Suddenly, she became a minor celebrity in local churches. She spoke of her past in lurid detail and described the way she had been saved. Parents and pastors pointed proudly to this young woman as an outstanding example of the power of the Gospel. Her fame spread to neighboring counties. Meanwhile, she announced her plans to become an evangelist. Several weeks later, however, store detectives caught her stuffing a handful of lipsticks into her purse.

She tearfully confessed, "I thought when I was saved that I'd never be tempted again."

As a matter of fact, the moments of highest vision seem to be followed by the times of greatest peril. God's call is often followed by a clash. The Lord does not seem to want us to stay perpetually on a peak of spirituality.

How well I remember the time I appeared before the elders of the church to state that I was called to be a minister. I was eighteen years old. It was a moving experience for me. I shared my imperfect understanding of the Christian faith, and the elders prayed for me. I felt a sense of achievement and exaltation when I left. I would be a minister! As I strutted from the church that evening, I preened myself on acting so adult and I gloried in being so humble! I fancied myself a hero because I was accepted as a minister-to-be.

I walked into our house in a mild state of euphoria. The first thing I noticed, however, was my kid sister wearing an old shirt of mine. Suddenly, I exploded in wrath. My shirt! I excoriated her angrily for taking that old shirt without my permission. I denounced her for every real or imagined sin she had ever committed against me or the entire human race. I filled the air with nasty words and bitter feelings. My petulant, childish outburst was *anything* but Christian or ministerial. I learned early that God's call does not mean an end to testing and temptation. In fact, God's call seems to lead to testing and temptation.

The Temptation of Jesus

This was Jesus' experience also. Immediately after His baptism and call, He was driven out into the wilderness and into a period of temptation. He had no lasting spiritual jag, no permanent glow of a born-again experience. The summons led to a struggle.

At His baptism, Jesus had understood God's message to Him to be: "Take my love to others, and love them until You die for them. Bring in my realm of *shalom* and conquer all resistance to my caring, not with power, but by sacrificing. Sacrifice for them. Suffer with them and hurt for them. Keep at it, even though it will lead to a cross."

Satan's message to Jesus was, "It's foolish. You'll only be frustrated. Ultimately, loving like that is futile. You will fail. You must listen to me. I have sensible advice."

Do you remember Jesus' temptations? Each temptation made such good sense!

The first temptation was to turn stones into bread. What a superb idea! Satan was whispering, in effect: "Get your program off the ground. Take care of people's needs immediately. After all, taking care of the hungry is good. Besides, you are hungry, so take care of yourself."

Jesus' second temptation was to leap from the temple pinnacle and land safely in the street below. What a sensation that would create! Satan hissed words to the effect of "How this will make headlines! People will hear about you and believe you're Mister Somebody. You'll get results. You'll prove yourself instantly."

The third temptation Satan threw at Jesus was to organize a superstate. "Be a generalissimo!" Satan cunningly said. "Bring in God's realm the way the world understands: a mighty power. For the good of the world, push everyone into the kingdom. After all, you know what's best for folks, don't you?"

Jesus continued to go through testing and struggle to the very end. Powers opposing God tried to thwart Jesus throughout His ministry. Satan continued his onslaught. When Peter tried to dissuade Jesus from going to Jerusalem, Jesus spoke sternly, recognizing the voice: "Get behind me, Satan!" (Mark 8:33). In the Gethsemane scene, Jesus agonized in prayer about escaping the cross. On the cross itself, Jesus hears the taunts to save Himself and prove who He claims to be by coming down from the cross. It is not until the Resurrection that Jesus triumphs. Only as the risen Lord does Jesus emerge from struggle, testing and temptation by Satan. The power of Satan is greater than our wildest guess, but Jesus outlasted it.

The Adversary

Let's talk for a moment about this term *Satan*. Perhaps you have the same picture I used to have whenever the word Satan was used: a notion of a rather comic figure with horns, forked tail, silly grin, wearing red tights and carrying a pitchfork. The cartoonists have managed to render Satan harmless. In the Bible, the term is used to refer to an opponent. The word meant "adversary" in the original use. The New Testament invariably uses the article to speak of "the satan" or the adversary.

In other words, you will struggle with your adversary

through the rest of your life, once you have understood something of God's realm and God's plans for you. Your adversary will try to deflect you from being God's person and from doing God's work.

Your adversary is cleverer than you imagine. Your adversary will take many forms, because he is a genius at disguises. The name for Satan is also "the father of lies," because he comes so cunningly and can deceive so convincingly. Your adversary knows your weaknesses better than anyone except God. The adversary always sounds so reasonable. He makes such good sense. He speaks so convincingly. And the adversary sneaks up when you think you are safest in the arms of God.

In one of the lurid sections of the Book of Revelation (9:1–10), there is a description of some enormous locusts that plague nonbelievers in the last days. These great grasshoppers from hell swarm everywhere and threaten to destroy everyone not marked by the sign of God. These locusts are understood to be symbols of temptation. They have bodies like horses, showing how temptations are powerful, even stronger than men. These locusts also have faces like men, revealing how rational and plausible temptations always are. They have the beautiful hair of a lovely woman, describing how attractive temptations are. Finally, these locusts have tails like scorpions, showing how temptations always have a hidden deadly sting.

At times we are all surrounded by the locust swarm of temptations. They are always stronger than we imagine. They are always so plausible, so enticing. The sting is not apparent at first, but the effects of temptation are always painful, sometimes lethal.

The adversary Satan comes to some in the form of friends and slogans, as to a college student who has some lingering childhood sense of being a Christian but is starting to sort out values on his own. "If it feels good, it's good," the adversary assures him. The voice of the adversary comes through persuasively from conversations with buddies who espouse the *Playboy* philosophy, through magazines, through many films and television shows.

Here is a young executive. She has some ideals and creativity. She attributes these to the Spirit of God prompting her to do something valuable with her life. She considered social work and the Peace Corps as well as a business career, but the adversary whispers, "Look out for yourself. No one else will. Assert yourself. Express yourself. Be comfortable. Build up some security for yourself. Enjoy yourself." The adversary coos convincing words every time she gets her paycheck or hears friends at lunch report on trips to the islands or relaxes after a tennis game with companions.

I once heard of a minister in the north of England who preached a sermon with the title "The Temptations of Milkmen." I still have not figured out how he could devote an entire sermon on the peculiar pitfalls suffered by those delivering milk, but I have to admit the preacher recognized that the adversary has unique temptations for each profession. Milkmen have their own temptations. And so do preachers!

Each age has its own assaults by the adversary. "Young fellows are tempted by girls," wrote Martin Luther. "Men who are thirty years old are tempted by gold. When they are forty years old they are tempted by honor and glory. And those who are sixty years old say to themselves, 'What a pious man I have become!' "

In a talk to Cambridge undergraduates before his death a few years ago, C. S. Lewis said, "The most compelling of all temptations is the temptation to the inner circle. Men will lie, betray their wives for admission to the circle. . . . The charm of the inner circle lies in the fact that others may not enter, that only a select few are admitted."

That was the trouble with some of the bright young men

on the White House staff during the Watergate era. The
game of being in the inner circle became more important
than anything else. It became an end.

"Somewhere between my ambition and my ideals, I lost
my ethical compass," Jeb Stuart Magruder confessed before
being sentenced for his Watergate role. "I found myself on a
path that had not been intended for me by my parents or my
principles or by my own ethical instincts. It has led me to this
courtroom."

The adversary hurls temptations at us from without. These
fall under the category of "London" temptations and require
"London grace" according to old John Newton, author of
such hymns as "Amazing Grace."

> London is a dangerous and ensnaring place. I account my-
> self happy that my lot is cast at a distance from it. . . . I often
> think of the difference between London grace and country
> grace. By London grace, when genuine, I understand grace in
> a very advanced degree. The favoured few who are kept alive
> to God, simple-hearted and spiritually-minded, in the first-
> rate Christians of the land. Not that we are without our trials
> here. The evil of our own hearts and the devices of Satan cut
> us out work enough. My own soul is kept alive, as it were, by
> miracle. The enemy thrusts sore at me that I may fall. In
> London I am in a crowd of temptations, but in the country
> there is a crowd of temptations in me. To what purpose do I
> boast of retirement, when I am myself possessed of Satan's le-
> gions in every place? My mind, even at Olney, is a perfect
> puppet-show, a Vanity Fair, an absolute Newgate itself.
>
> *Cardiphonia*

The Crowd of Temptations in Me

For some, inner temptation is the temptation to think
you'll never be tempted. Or it may be temptation to imagine
that you will never be conquered by any temptation.

Before World War II, France built an immense series of

fortifications along its border with Germany. The French dubbed this carefully constructed series of deep tunnels, bunkers, pillboxes and antitank barricades the Maginot Line. The French government haughtily assumed that German forces would never be able to invade France. Few Frenchmen were prepared for the shock when Hitler's *Luftwaffe* flew *over* the impregnable Maginot Line, parachuted troops inside France and conquered France within weeks.

Maginot Line mentality pervades Christian thinking, too. The adversary sometimes leapfrogs over our vaunted defenses and conquers us unexpectedly. The person who boasts, "Well, at least that is one thing *I* would never do," is going to be caught napping behind that Maginot Line. History is full of castles captured just when the defenders thought they were safe and needed no guard. Nothing gives temptation a better chance than overconfidence. At our weakest and strongest points, we must be on watch.

Good intentions are not enough. Nor is willpower. To stand up to the assaults of the adversary, we need more than grit and resolve.

Remember Peter? On the night Jesus was arrested, Peter had boasted he could stand up to any problem. Jesus warned him that he would be tempted, but Peter brushed aside Jesus' words. He grabbed his sword, certain that he could face anything. Peter's downfall came when a servant girl asked questions about his ties with Jesus. The blustery superman who had bragged he could handle any temptation could not face the scorn of some bystanders. It was too tempting to deny any relationship with Jesus. A cocky Peter became a contrite Peter.

Being a Christian means you will struggle more with the adversary than your non-Christian friends. You are sensitive to the way God wants this world to be, therefore you are at odds with the way the adversary tries to make the world into less than God intends. Perhaps you have been experiencing a sense of the conflict Jesus felt in the wilderness and through-out His ministry. You have been trying to work for peace in the face of an insane arms race and threatening escalation of American involvement in Central America, or you have been trying to meet the needs of the poor, homeless and hungry in your city. And you have encountered apathy among most and hostility among many. You feel alone. You feel deserted. You wonder what the point of struggling and ministering may be when so little seems to be accomplished.

Sometimes that voice of the adversary comes through people you love. You hear friends or loved ones advising you to back off. "Why bother?" you hear, hissing in your ears along with the cries from the oppressed saying, "Please bother!" You feel despair and depression. You are at the point of quitting. You tell yourself in these moments that maybe the world is right when it says to live the good life by looking after yourself and working to be successful and comfortable.

This assault by the adversary came to Jesus also. The adversary, the satan, tried to deflect Him from His ministry by advising Him it was useless and hopeless—that all He'd get for His efforts would be loneliness and rejection, tears and pain. Through Peter's voice, the adversary urged Jesus not to bother risking His life by going to Jerusalem. Jesus sternly told off the adversary trying to use Peter.

Today the adversary continues his insidiously clever and powerful attacks on each of us. He tries to seduce us from carrying out what the Lord intends us to be. He tries to deflect us from serving others. But Jesus bore His cross. He calls us to bear ours.

The final—and worst—temptation is to give up on God. Or, the obverse side of that temptation: being tempted to think that God has given up on you.

Jesus faced this temptation in His dying hours. He gasped

these words: ". . . My God, my God, why hast thou forsaken me?" (Matthew 27:46; Mark 15:34.)

Have you ever felt God deserted you? Have you ever thought, "What can God do?" Have you ever felt your faith crumbling as you tried to cope? Have circumstances threatened to overwhelm you, making you feel that God was distant or absent? Have you been ready to quit?

The Gospel of Jesus Christ is the Good News that God is stronger than the adversary. Christ's power sustains you through *any* temptation! He promises to deliver us from the destructive grip of each assault of the tempter. The risen, living Lord stands with you in the midst of every time of testing!

In A.D. 563 on the Isle of Iona, off the bleak western coast of Scotland, a missionary named Columba landed from Ireland to bring the Gospel to the wild, uncivilized highlanders and islanders inhabiting northern Scotland. Columba had left the pleasant surroundings of life in the court in Ireland, which at that time was the intellectual and spiritual capital of Europe. Columba knew he would face terrible opposition, possibly death, from the savage heathen.

Looking around him, he realized how forsaken he was. He knew he would be lonely and frightened. Columba also knew that the trials of serving would cause him to be tempted to sail back to the warmth and lights of his beloved homeland. What were the first things he did? He prayed. Next, he buried his boat. Columba knew he would be tempted to quit, but he had confidence that the ever-present God would strengthen him to stand up to any trials. He took immediate steps to make sure he would rely on God during his trials.

In our temptations, we must remember that we are never left alone. God is in it with us. We must never think we must depend only on our frail resources. In fact, we must have a "bury the boat" kind of trust in Him!

8

He Gives Us
New Beginnings

There is a small museum in Norton, Kansas, that is dedicated to perpetuating the memories of defeated candidates for the office of president of the United States. Not surprisingly, it's a rather pathetic affair and does not attract much interest. Failure is not popular.

Ask any candidate who has lost an election. Ask any coach whose team has an 0–7 record. Ask the person who tried to start his own business and has been squeezed into bankruptcy. Ask the Iowa farmer who lost his farm due to low farm prices and ruinous costs. Ask the person recently divorced. Defeat is not easy.

Our culture calls for winning; we have no philosophy for failure. Defeat is contrary to everything sacred in our society. To be defeated is to be disgraced. To be defeated is to be nobody. "America," says Ross McWhirter, *The Guinness Book of Records* editor, "is the most competitive nation in the world. That's why out of ten thousand entries, thirty percent are Americans."

Take sports. We are experts at winning, but amateurs at losing. The noble loser may be part of the British tradition, but not the American. The Vince Lombardi principle applies to American culture: "Winning isn't eveything; it's the only thing," and we are made to sense that failure in any form is disreputable.

Yet you will have to live with some failures. Regardless of who you are, you will sense the dull ache of being made to feel like a worthless failure at some time. Occasionally, defeat will bring a sharp pain.

I have a friend who started out to be a missionary doctor but got sidetracked by the war, then decided to make some money, marry and raise his family. He kept telling himself that someday he would answer the call to complete his medical studies and offer to serve overseas in a backward, needy area. It's too late now, and he lives with the painful memory of not fulfilling what he feels God had called him to do.

I was made to feel like a useless, worthless failure in the primary grades by the subject then known as penmanship. My problems in penmanship started with the fact that I am left-handed. The arrangement of the desk, with the inkwell in the upper right-hand corner; the position of the paper at a certain slant; the very writing instrument, a wooden holder with steel pen point, held in my fist in an inverted position— everything conspired against me. Teachers tried to get me to write properly by using my right hand, but, having failed, resigned themselves to having to work with an obstinate and clumsy pupil.

My efforts to bring pen from inkwell to paper were disastrous. My left hand smeared the ink. The freshly inscribed lines turned into dark blue-black smudges. Occasionally, the pen tip scratched the paper, spattering ink droplets. My sweeping practice figures always became soiled blotches instead of graceful Spencerian strokes. I felt like a failure in penmanship.

Undoubtedly you had painful times in adolescence when feelings of being worth little surfaced. The memories are still present. Our culture says you don't amount to much if you're not physically attractive, youthfully energetic, sexually active, perpetually successful. But the adversary, the evil one, the tempter, the accuser tries to destroy you by convincing you how useless and worthless you are.

If you are a woman in your forties or early fifties, you have been made to feel guilty because you have not gone back to school for a graduate degree or haven't gone out and gotten a job.

If you are handicapped, in our society you are still discriminated against or made to feel you are less than a human being because you are physically limited in certain ways. Because you are in a wheelchair, you think you are a worthless failure.

If you are a person who lost someone very special to you, you keep reminding yourself that you noticed the symptoms and should have urged the other to get medical attention earlier. Now it's too late, and you blame yourself.

General Jonathan Wainwright, who held out on Corregidor before being forced to surrender during the bleak days of 1942, felt he was a worthless failure for three long years in Japanese prisoner-of-war camps. When he was finally released from the stockade in Manchuria and brought to MacArthur's headquarters, at first he was too ashamed to speak. He had gone through the terrible sifting of defeat and felt disgrace for having surrendered.

The disciple Peter also knew failure. Peter was warned by Jesus that he would have such times. "Simon, Simon," Jesus says, using his old name. "Satan has demanded to have all of you sifted" (*see* Luke 22:31). Jesus used vivid words describing a farmer in the Middle East violently shaking and tossing the grain through a sieve, so that only the worthless bits of stubble, sticks and gravel are left.

Peter, you will remember, pooh-poohs the idea, insisting that he is ready to go anywhere with Jesus. "Nothing will ever make me feel like a worthless failure," Peter announces. Jesus quietly replies that before the sound of the rooster the following morning, Peter will be sifted. That evening, the sifting comes unexpectedly. A girl who works in the high priest's house quizzes Peter about being a follower of the prisoner inside, and Peter heatedly and repeatedly denies any association with Jesus. Just then, the cock crows, Jesus is led out, and Peter sees Jesus' look. A sense of being a worthless failure suddenly overwhelms him. He rushes out, leans his head in his hands and weeps.

You know the feeling.

If you do, God assures you that He offers you new life. You may assume that you need not bother anymore with God, or with life or with yourself. However, the Lord *insists* on bothering with you! With Him, your life is never a failure. The living One stands with you in love and patience.

The great Italian artist Michelangelo once saw a chunk of worthless marble waiting to be discarded from a builder's yard. Michelangelo said to the builder, "Take it to the studio! There's an angel in there, and I can set it free!"

Be confident! Although you may give up on yourself, God has not. You may see only worthless junk and think you are only fit to be thrown on the discard pile, but through Jesus Christ, God has come to bring you hope for yourself and your future! He wants to free the angel in you!

Failure's Benefits

With Jesus Christ, we learn that failure is a great teacher. Tasting defeat can help us equip ourselves to cope better with the difficulties that inevitably face us in life.

European historians unanimously agree that if Napoleon had suffered at least one substantial defeat earlier in his military career, he would not have brashly tried to march to Moscow in the winter, incurring a disastrous defeat for the French army.

Compare Napoleon to Dwight D. Eisenhower, who had allowed failure to be his teacher. General Eisenhower, aware of the possibility of failure on D-Day, June 6, 1944, privately prepared a dispatch he carried in his wallet:

> Our landings in the Cherbourg-Havre area have failed to gain a satisfactory foothold and I have withdrawn the troops. My decision to attack at this time and place was based on the best information available. The troops, the air, and the Navy did all that bravery and devotion to duty could do. If any blame or fault attaches to the attempt it is mine alone.

A half-century ago, the great chess player José Capablanca stated, "Nothing is so healthy as a thrashing at the proper time, and from very few won games have I learned as much as I have from most of my defeats."

I have to learn this lesson again and again. For example, one week I came down with a severe case of laryngitis and an upper-respiratory infection. In thirty-five years of preaching as a pastor, I had never failed to preach when scheduled. Although I had been mildly under the weather a couple of times, I had always managed to tough it out.

I confess that I had a bit of a superman complex. At times I also secretly felt that because I was to be about church work, God would not dare let me miss a Sunday preaching appointment. The universe revolved on my being in my pulpit robe at 8:30 and 11:00 A.M.! Then came that infection and hoarseness that would not disappear for several days.

On Sunday, I was depressed. When I tried to analyze it, I began to understand that I was actually suffering from a sense of failure. I had been licked! I had committed the unpardonable sin of suffering defeat. As God used a Persian king named Cyrus to be His instrument (*see* Isaiah 45), so I began to comprehend He could use a throat virus to bring a proud preacher to his senses.

One day, a dejected young writer interviewed Thomas J. Watson, president and guiding genius of IBM. The young man told Watson he was failing in his attempts to be a writer.

Watson replied, "You're making a common mistake. You're thinking of failure as the enemy of success. But it isn't at all. Failure is a teacher—a harsh one, but the best.

"You say you have a desk full of rejected manuscripts? That's great! Every one of those manuscripts was rejected for a reason. Have you pulled them to pieces looking for that reason?"

Here is the outline of the career of one person who used failure as a teacher for faith. He failed in business when he was twenty-two. He was defeated the following year when he ran for the legislature. He failed in business a second time the year after that. He was finally elected the following year to the legislature, but when he was twenty-nine, he suffered a nervous breakdown. Everyone wrote him off as a man who didn't have what it took. Two years later, he was defeated for speaker of the legislature; two years after that, soundly defeated as a state elector. He was defeated when he was thirty-four for land officer, then the same year defeated for Congress. Two years later, he was defeated for Congress; two years after that, defeated a *third time* for Congress. A few years later, defeated for Senate; the following year, defeated for the vice-presidential nomination; two years later, defeated for Senate.

But in 1860, this man was elected the sixteenth president of the United States. Abraham Lincoln had failed repeatedly and picked up a reputation as a loser. He was beaten to his knees time and time again. But out of all this, he gained the strength that carried a nation during its most critical years.

The greatest lesson failure can teach is that God is supreme. Our failures may be used as reminders that *we* are not supreme, God is. However, we want to dictate to God; we want to lay down the terms; we want to give the orders. We want Him to be the listener.

God is sovereign. We must come to terms with Him—on His terms. "Our real business is business with God," as Calvin said. And that means understanding He is always at work in human affairs, even in those times we call defeats. In times of defeat, He frequently is doing more than we ever fathom.

Who would have dared imagine that in 540 B.C. in the worst days of the exile under the Babylonian king Cyrus, who did not know God, Darius the Persian was being prepared by God to be His instrument. Who would have dared imagine that at the cross, at the total defeat of the life and career of Jesus (by our standards), God would take the nail-pierced corpse in a grave as His instrument of resurrection?

Rejoice! God is never intimidated. God is able. He is not helpless, He rules supreme. Because He reigns for ever and ever, we can live with any defeat without despairing. Even death need not be seen as hopeless defeat with God, since we know He has already dealt with Jesus' death and our deaths.

I recall meeting two Anglican missionaries in a remote part of India a few years ago. They had built a small chapel and school. The two had lived in the village for ten years, but they had not made any converts. A visitor asked them if they didn't feel discouraged because of their failure to make any villagers Christian after so long in India. "Failure? Discouraged?" answered one gentleman of faith. "What is ten years in the history of God's Church?"

We may fail. We may be defeated, but not God! God is at work. History may be the record of human folly and confusion, but it is also the story of the Lord's activity and concern. God is supreme!

The news that gives you a future with hope, in spite of your despair over the past, is realizing that Jesus has prayed for you and is praying for you now. In the Greek New Testament, the words of His assurance are emphatic and leap out at the reader: *I am praying for you.* If Jesus is praying for you, even when you feel you are a worthless failure, you know you have worth and you realize that you have a future. The past is over, and God creates all things new, including your life. "If God be for us, who can be against us?" (*See* Romans 8:31.)

Pray! God is at work in His universe. Pray with confidence and persistence. Archbishop William Temple used to say, "When I pray, coincidences happen. When I don't, they don't."

In God's eyes, the only failure that is a sin is realizing what God intends and refusing to do it. "Whoever knows what is right to do and fails to do it," writes James, "for him it is sin" (James 4:17).

Your task and mine as the Church is to share that power of Christ that steadies us. As John Baillie of Edinburgh used to say, "The congregation exists to do in the parish what Jesus would do were He still in the flesh." Our congregations are intended to be parts of Christ's extended family, bringing security, support and healing to each member.

Sharing Christ's power within that family means never putting anyone down. Standing as His sisters and brothers calls for building one another up. Society and our culture delight in cutting people up and disposing of them as failures. But not Christians. Those gifted with Christ's mercy seek to humanize every institution. They try to inject an awareness of other people into every arena of human existence. They give imaginative attention to brothers and sisters in the ghettos of our area and nation, and to the two-thirds of the human race who know only hunger, poverty and disease for themselves and their children.

You see, anyone who is reflecting the steadying presence of Jesus is never a worthless failure. She or he is a mini-Christ for others, and in God's scheme, that spells usefulness and significance, now and forevermore!

9

Basing Our
Decisions on Him

An old tale from the Jewish *Talmud* describes what it's like to have to make decisions and not always be sure what is right. It seems that two young rabbis were talking one day with the great sage Rabbi Isaac Napcha. The first young rabbi, Reb Ami, asked the wise old teacher, "Tell us, sir, some pretty legend."

But the second young rabbi, Reb Assi, said, "No, rather explain to us some nice point of the law."

When the teacher began the legend he displeased the one, and when he began to explain a point of law he offended the other. Whereupon he took up this parable: "I am like the

man with the two wives, the one young and the other old.
The young one plucked out all his gray hairs, that he might
look young; the old wife pulled out all his black hairs, that he
might look old; and so between the two, he became bald. So
it is with me between you."

You are sometimes put in the position of having to make
tough choices, and you aren't always certain that you're
making the correct decision.

An attorney is representing a man who is owed a consider-
able sum by a small plumber. The plumber cannot pay his
debt because he has been careless in collecting from his debt-
ors. The lawyer faces a dilemma: Should she bring suit
against the plumber, which she knows will put the plumber
out of business? Or should she consider the hardship she will
cause the plumber and not bring charges, which would, in
turn, adversely affect her client?

A manager knows he should lay off some employees. To do
so, of course, would work hardship on these people and their
families. It would also work hardship on the community and
local businesses. On the other hand, to not lay them off would
not be looking after the interests of the company, its owners
and stockholders, and would jeopardize the interests of customers, suppliers, other employees and the community at
large. What should be his decision?

Deciding what is right and wrong is not simple. Furthermore, whatever choice you make is often going to cause
someone—you or others—some pain.

Some years ago, an outbreak of cholera threatened the
people of Manila. A young American public health official,
Dr. Victor G. Heiser, insisted on burning the huts where
cholera had been discovered. Although denounced and opposed by many in the Philippines for his stern measures, the
doctor insisted that medical reasons compelled him to burn
the huts.

Shortly afterward, a fisherman in Manila Bay noticed a
streak in the water in the shape of a cross. Tasting, the fisher-

man found the water was sweet, not salty. A priest was rowed out to the place and pronounced it a miracle. Soon people began to row out and fill bottles with the miraculous water.

Heiser, however, discovered that a break had occurred in a sewer. He appealed to the militia to prevent the populace from drinking the contaminated water floating in the "miraculous" place in the bay. He was told that the people were already angry at losing their huts through his measures and might riot if prevented from enjoying the waters from the "miracle." Heiser was denounced by the priests. Standing for truth, Heiser made his decision to risk a riot rather than an epidemic. He endured unpopularity, but his decision saved hundreds of lives.

Decision making does not come easily!

How *Not* to Make Decisions

How do you go about making the right decision? Do you *pass the buck*? Let others make the decision for you?

Tea is never served at the Gypsy Tea Kettle on New York's Lexington Avenue, but most afternoons men and women in business suits sit at small cafe tables waiting for a fifteen-minute "psychic reading." They are part of an enormous group of devotees who consult psychics, tarot card readers, astrologers and numerologists. Whether simply tossing a coin and making a decision on the basis of heads or tails or paying coins to someone claiming ESP knowledge, the idea is the same: Evade making the decision yourself. Let someone else do it. The neat thing about this dodge is that you can always put the blame on the person who gave you the advice, in case things don't turn out well.

Of course you can always try *putting off making a decision*. "Decide later" is sometimes good advice, but it also can be a nice way of allowing yourself to procrastinate.

Artist William Hunt was once coaching a class of dabblers trying to paint a sunset. He noticed one pupil working care-

fully on the details of the shingles of an old shed in the land-
scape, while ignoring the western sky. "Son," said Hunt, "it
won't be light long. You haven't time for shingles *and* sunsets.
You must choose."

You discover that you have only limited time, and you
cannot put off the decision to paint the sunset too long.

Maybe you handle the hard choices by *avoiding a decision*
and saying, "Well, it doesn't make any difference which way
I go. What I decide is so insignificant."

Have you never heard of the power of just one vote? It was
one vote that gave Oliver Cromwell control of England in
1656. It was one vote that gave America English instead of
the German language in 1776. It was one vote that changed
France from a monarchy into a republic in 1875. It was one
vote that gave the presidency of the United States to Ruther-
ford B. Hayes in 1876. And it was one vote that gave Adolf
Hitler leadership of the Nazi party in Germany in 1923.

In each of these cases, just one person made a decision that
had incalculable consequences!

You may have the idea that you can work out your decision
making satisfactorily by *merely staying within the law.* "If
it's legal, it's okay," you say.

A friend of mine told me how he discovered he could not
base his decisions only on making sure he was not breaking
any laws.

Ed was in charge of purchasing land in a distant city for his
business firm. He traveled to the other city, found a licensed
real estate broker, and spent many days with the real estate
man checking out various locations for commercial purposes.
The available lots were all either too large or too small, except one parcel of land. This piece of real estate was too expensive.

A few days later, the owner of the high-priced lot called
Ed, offering to sell. Ed asked if he'd come down in price.

"Well, you might say that," replied the owner. "I figure

my land is worth five hundred thousand dollars, plus the seven percent for the real estate commission, which makes it five hundred thirty-five thousand dollars. You don't have a contract with the real estate agent, so I'll act as my own agent and save you the thirty-five thousand dollar commission. How about it?"

Ed asked, "But what about all the time—the hours and hours—the real estate man put in trying to help me? He was the guy who located your piece of property. It's hardly fair to him."

The owner laughed. "He has no legal recourse. It's all part of the game."

Ed refused to take advantage of a conscientious real estate agent to pull a shrewd deal. Decisions that are right sometimes come hard and often cost!

You may be one of those who have the fuzzy solution of deciding what to do by telling yourself that anything you decide is fine *as long as it's for a good cause.* Maybe it is sometimes, but not always.

A family was on vacation in a remote area in sparsely populated northern Minnesota. The father went off for a few days' fishing, leaving the family in a small resort. Calling the family a couple of days after leaving, the father learned that his little boy was severely ill with a high fever and sore throat. He asked if the doctor had been called. The father was told the doctor was away visiting relatives over the weekend, but had promised to come at once.

The father left immediately. Driving along a back road, his car stalled. In desperation, he ran and walked to the nearest town, praying with every step that someone might pick him up. When he came to the main road, he saw a filling station. A car was standing by the pump. In a frenzy, he jumped into the car and drove wildly home. He even thanked God for supplying him a way. When he arrived home and found the boy still alive, he thanked God.

The son was dangerously ill. An hour passed and the doctor still had not come. The son gasped for breath and died. When the doctor finally came, he told the father how sorry he was. Had he been there, he could have saved the boy from choking to death by performing a tracheotomy. Then he told the father the reason for the delay: Someone had stolen his car at the gas station.

Some well-meaning people try to solve decision-making dilemmas by twisting the Christian faith into a sort of "Dial-an-Answer." They have the mistaken notion that there is a simple, pat answer to everything. Some, for example, mistakenly think the Bible is a sort of super answer book where you can look up a solution. They would have you believe the Bible is carefully catalogued, tabulated and cross-indexed. *"Look it up in the Bible"* may sound pious, but it is not very practical. Nor is it using the Bible the right way.

Others think prayer will give a quick, easy answer. Again, this sounds pious. In reality, however, it is reducing prayer to the level of those machines in amusement parks and drugstores where you drop a penny in the slot and get your weight and fortune printed on a card. *Penny-in-the-slot prayers* for quick answers are just as silly.

"Follow your conscience," someone says. Yes, but conscience can be terribly misleading. Never forget that Hitler claimed to be following his conscience. So did Pontius Pilate the day he delivered Jesus to be crucified. It is not enough to tell someone to do right or be good.

"Do just what Jesus would do," someone else says. This sounds fine. It is sound advice in a general sense, for Jesus is our model. However, it is no help on specific problems. For example, what did Jesus ever say about corporation tax structures? Furthermore, when people tried to make Jesus an expert on human affairs and problems, He always refused. He would never do another person's thinking for him. In Luke

12:14, Jesus emphatically asks a man trying to push Him into being an arbiter of a family squabble, "Who made me a judge?"

We will not find easy answers through making the Bible, prayer, conscience or Jesus into an answer machine. There is no hot line to heaven. When we act as if there is, we are apt to slip into trying to manipulate God for our purposes.

Jesus Is the Answer

Jesus Christ does not come through with nifty solutions to every decision, but He is the key to all decision making. The decision behind every decision must always be: "Jesus is Lord! I will try to be faithful to Him as Lord in this set of circumstances." When we have difficult decisions to make and are not sure what is right, we start by consciously deciding again that we belong to Him and are called to be responsible to Him.

Commit yourself to Jesus Christ.

This means turning yourself in the right general direction. It means making the fundamental decision of your life to put yourself on the Lord's side. It means putting yourself in a position to know God's will.

Jesus is the norm by which everyone and everything in life is measured. He is the criterion for what we believe and how we act. He says, "I am the way, and the truth, and the life . . ." (John 14:6). He claims to be the final authority. He insists that we examine our goals and acts and values and thoughts in the light of whether or not these conform to Him. When we base our lives on Him as the truth, we discover we are able to make decisions in a context that offers hope and direction.

An astronomer who is studying a star must continuously keep re-aiming his telescope, otherwise the earth's turning will put the star he is watching out of range. At each part of our lives, we must get fresh bearings on Jesus Christ. Other-

wise the changing situations we find ourselves in will put
Him out of focus and soon out of sight. Are we carefully and
continuously re-aiming our lives toward Christ?

The code room of the communications systems for the
C.I.A.'s spy satellites has been carefully designed to prevent
any unfriendly foreign agent from breaking in to steal secrets.
Yet materials from the code room (or "black vault") got into
the hands of Soviet agents. How?

A bright, sensitive young man named Christopher Boyce,
who had never had any trouble with the law and whose father was a career F.B.I. man, was in charge of the code room.
He and a friend named Andrew Daulton Lee decided to con-
spire against their government, and for two years photo-
graphed secret material from the "black vault" early in the
morning and late at night, then passed on the negatives to
Soviet operatives in Mexico City.

In spite of all the precautions and in spite of steel and con-
crete around the code room, the moral deterioration of Boyce
and Lee allowed national secrets to be taken to an unfriendly
nation. This is a reminder that our real security is based on
people's decisions. People, in turn, are reliable only when
they decide under an awareness of being God's. And they act
morally only when they live in trust and obedience before the
Lord. Christopher Boyce and Andrew Lee had brains, background—everything, it seems—except that sense of morality
resting on faith! The harvest of their unbelief has cost their
countrymen dearly.

Contrast the way these greedy people made fateful decisions to the way Robert E. Lee made his. At the close of the
Civil War, Robert E. Lee was financially ruined. He desperately needed a good job to pay off debts and support his family. Lee was approached by an insurance company that
offered him twenty-five thousand dollars a year as its president if he would allow the company to use his name. Lee
pointed out that he knew nothing about the insurance business. He was informed that the company did not want him to

take part in the business, but simply wanted to trade on his reputation as a promotional gimmick. Lee declined. Instead, he chose to accept the presidency of a small, struggling college at the paltry salary of fifteen hundred dollars per year. His decision did not earn him much security or fortune. Robert E. Lee, however, left his imprint on the lives of hundreds of young men.

A priest once met a man who got involved in corruption, and after being rebuked by the priest, the man claimed, "You don't know what the outside pressure was."

Indignantly, the priest declared, "Outside pressure, outside pressure! Where were your inner braces?"

Rabbi Balfour Brickner of the Stephen Wise Free Synagogue wrote, "Self-discipline, not externally applied discipline, is the only avenue to morality. It is what individuals do when alone, when no one is looking and when they know they won't get caught, that makes the difference between a civilization and a jungle."

Making tough decisions means more than having good intentions. Good decision making demands Christian commitment as its starting place. Otherwise you will be a person, as Theodore Roosevelt once said of William Howard Taft, "who means well feebly."

"Who Do You Say That I Am?"

This is your basic decision. Is Jesus your Lord and your Savior in every set of circumstances? This is the seminal choice of life. All other decisions depend on how you answer Jesus' question: "What do you decide about Me? Who do you say that I am when you're at work on Monday? What am I to you when nobody is looking and nobody will ever know?" Only when you have taken the definite step of enlisting to serve Him will you be able to begin to know and carry out God's will.

You must allow Him to communicate that will. This means

reading the Bible in the way it was intended: not as an answer book filled with cute tips and simple solutions, but as the unique and authoritative record of God's master plan. In and through Scripture, by the inspiration of the Holy Spirit, the Lord communicates with you. He speaks still. To use a military analogy, the Bible discloses God's overall strategy and plan of attack. The day-by-day skirmishing is left up to you. But the Spirit helps you to fit those day-by-day operations into the big scheme of things.

Seiji Ozawa, the conductor of the Boston Symphony, was rehearsing the Tanglewood orchestra one Saturday morning. A friend of mine sat quietly in the auditorium, enjoying the music.

He was puzzled, however, when a little man got up from the audience and walked up to the platform and whispered something to Ozawa, and even more puzzled that the great Ozawa stopped the rehearsal to let this little man interrupt him. This happened another time, and still a third time. Why, wondered my friend, would Ozawa permit this member of the audience to break into his conducting like that? Later my friend found out who the little man was. He was the composer of the piece. Ozawa humbly wanted to learn the way the master intended the piece to be performed. Great and famous though Seiji Ozawa is, he heeded the whispers. Only then could his decisions in leading the orchestra be consistent with what the composer intended.

So with us in our listening through Scripture meditation to the whispers of the Lord. We catch hints of the divine will in our decision making.

We know well how easy it is to substitute our will for God's will. We know our motives are always mixed. We know our grasp of the facts and our faith are never complete. "We know in part and we prophesy in part."

We face our tough decisions and make them as best we can, seeking to know God's will. We make them knowing they are not good decisions, and that even when we think we may have an inkling of God's will, we still will be mixing our will with the divine will.

We will ultimately be thrown on the mercy of God.

But this is the great thing about the Christian Gospel! God still accepts and forgives us, in spite of our poor decisions. This is the meaning of the cross and Resurrection! ". . . while we were yet sinners Christ died for us" (Romans 5:8). Unloved and unlovable though we are through the choices we are forced to make, our God has loved us and promises He always will!

Living by God's grace, we are freed to take the risk of making decisions. We realize none of our decisions will be perfect, but the Lord accepts us and empowers us to act!

The Savior for all seasons always brings a new season. The old season of poor or bad decisions is never the final one with Jesus Christ. He continually bestows fresh beginnings for those who trust in His mercy.

10

We Are Cherished
For Who We Are

Ira Gershwin was the brother of George Gershwin. Although also a gifted composer, Ira lived under the immense shadow of George. One time, listening to the radio, he heard the announcer intone, "And now, here is a new song by the great George Gershwin and his lovely wife Ira." Even within his own family, Ira was a victim of the unintentional slight. His father could remember George's melodies, but always remembered Ira's song "Fascinating Rhythm" as "Fashion on the River."

Poor Ira! All his life he had to endure the role of being "the other one," of having to take second place to another.

One of the effects of playing second fiddle is feeling that you are less than a person in your own right. You are deprived of the dignity of being a human of importance, or you are granted importance only because of the person who overshadows you.

The late Bishop Francis McConnell had a younger brother Pat who was also a Methodist minister. Less renowned than his famous brother, the bishop, Pat McConnell used to laugh and say that he went through life as the victim of the "double handshake." Whenever he was introduced to a stranger, he would receive the normal, perfunctory greeting. Then someone would mention that Pat McConnell was the brother of the well-known bishop. The stranger would invariably brighten, stride back to Pat, grab his hand a second time, and shake it much more heartily than he had at first.

Andrew was also a victim of the "double handshake." Brother of Simon Peter, Andrew was eclipsed by his illustrious relative. Peter was the gifted orator, the born leader. Peter became famous and made the headlines. Comparing ordinary Andrew to the flamboyant Peter is like contrasting a streetlight to a skyrocket.

Nobody really likes being the second fiddle. Yet much of the time we must be just that. Most Americans work for others, many in large corporations where there is a carefully structured hierarchy of jobs. Inevitably a great many of us, capable men and women, are going to have to play second fiddle much of our working lives. Most of us are going to be overshadowed by someone higher up.

In Pittsburgh a few years ago, a man tried to telephone a friend who was vice-president of Nabisco. When he reached the switchboard operator, he gave his friend's name.

"Who?" replied the polite voice at National Biscuit.

The man repeated the name of his friend, then added, "He is vice-president."

"Which division?"

"Uh, I think that he's in the baking division."

"Is he in bread?" persisted the receptionist.

"Yes," answered the man. "I think he's in bread."

The voice at the Nabisco switchboard promptly inquired further, "White or whole wheat?"

Corporation life means living in the shadow of others higher up the corporate structure, and therefore playing second fiddle. As many men and women working in big companies know, the workweek becomes a Monday-to-Friday survival march and the workday becomes an effort to ward off a sense of boring anonymity.

Playing second fiddle can also produce despair. Our culture dictates that every man must become a president, a chief, a head man of some sort. Otherwise, he is dubbed a failure, a nonentity. The person playing second fiddle, we have been led to think, is not a success.

No one bothers to mention that there is room for only a handful of "big men." Most of us, like it or not, are going to be second fiddles because there is not enough room at the top.

A survey was made of a class of Harvard Business School graduates. Through their training, these persons were made to believe they would be classified as failures unless they were first in everything. The most unhappy and frustrated were those who were vice-presidents. These men and women felt acutely that they were dismal number twos. Their perception of themselves was that they were doomed to be pegged as second best. Feeling cheated by life, they allowed their resentment to stain their marriages, their family lives, their friendships, their health and their church relationships.

The Horatio Alger rules of hard work, frugality, and a big smile do not mean we inevitably end up at the top of the ladder. Many who followed the Horatio Alger advice find themselves still on the lower rungs at age fifty-five or sixty. More than one man has a deep sense of uneasiness over being a second fiddle; he feels guilty for "not working hard enough," "not succeeding."

More than one woman despairs over being overshadowed by others. For most women, marriage means putting her husband and children into prominence. Most wives and mothers automatically disqualify themselves from being a first fiddle. Only such a woman knows how much of her status, her freedom, her comforts, and her interests she has sacrificed for her family. Playing second fiddle seems to give some women a stigma. Too often, when a woman replies that she is "only a housewife," one has the feeling that she is really saying, "I haven't amounted to much, have I?"

Sometimes, we are forced to play second fiddle because of circumstances beyond our control. We are *almost* heroes or heroines. But for a sheriff's order, a man named Clarence D. Chamberlin might be better known than Charles A. Lindbergh.

Chamberlin was set to leave Roosevelt Field on Long Island, New York, for Germany weeks before Lindbergh took off on May 20, 1927, for his record-breaking flight to Paris. Chamberlin, however, had some financial difficulties resulting in a lawsuit. A sheriff's attachment kept his plane, *The Columbia*, tied to the ground. Fifteen days after Lindbergh's famous flight, Chamberlin cleared himself of the writ and did take off. He even set two records: He carried the first passenger on a nonstop trans-Atlantic flight and he established a new distance mark of 3,911 miles. Lindbergh, however, carried off the laurels and became the hero. Chamberlin was forced into a dismal second place.

When we are eclipsed by another, even the best of us may become jealous. An ancient fable from the early church in North Africa relates that the devil came across a group of lesser fiends trying to tempt a godly church father who was praying alone in the desert. The minor devils had tried unsuccessfully to divert the holy man with pleasant fleshly temptations. They had tried to work on the man's doubts and fears, but he withstood their attempts to undermine his faith.

The devil, according to the old tale, haughtily stepped forward and informed the junior tempters that their methods were crude. Addressing the devout old hermit who had withstood all the wiles of the other evil powers, the devil said, "Have you heard the news? Your brother has just been made bishop of Alexandria!" With that, the serene face of the venerable holy man was clouded by a scowl of jealousy.

We may feel as if we are merely number two. Or we may be reduced by our company or society to a series of coded numbers and letters in a computerized printout. We may live in the shadow of others and feel insignificant. We may even go through seasons of insignificance.

The Savior for all seasons, however, looks on you as one with value! God does not remember you as a number. Nor does the Lord regard you as a fraction of a total. Through Jesus Christ, God assures you that you are never a statistic with Him.

Your Gifts of the Spirit

In fact, you are unique. You are special. You have been given exceptional gifts by the Lord, to be shared with the others in Christ's community. Are you aware of these gifts?

When I was a boy, I believed there was a pecking order in the Church. I had my own notion of who outranked whom. Based on my youthful understanding of who was important in the congregation, I put together my flow chart for my church. It listed each congregational personality in order of importance. Topping the list, of course, was the minister. After all, he wore a badge of authority in the form of a robe for worship and carried the title Reverend. He outranked everyone.

Next, in my understanding of the power structure of our

congregation, stood Otto Bergmeyer. Otto Bergmeyer operated a barber shop across from the central fire station from Monday through Saturday, but on Sunday he was the imposing presence who directed the ushering and seating with a mighty dignity and graciousness.

That position in my little hierarchy was almost equaled by Lewis Baker, the high school principal who was the leading elder and could offer prayers in a voice that sounded like a minister's. Then came Maude Crain, the soprano soloist, then George Spitzer, teacher of the boys' Sunday-school class. But the bottom of the totem pole was reserved for Margaret Simpson.

Margaret Simpson was a short, plump widow. With her florid face, she looked like a little red fireplug in motion. She always seemed to be perspiring and always had strands of hair flopping over her forehead. But it was her smile, a perpetual toothless grin, that made some of us wise guys think Margaret was somewhat retarded. Some whispered that Margaret could barely write her name and couldn't read beyond the second-grade level. She sang so badly off-key that people instinctively tried to distance themselves from her in the church pew.

In my stupidity, I assumed that Margaret Simpson had the fewest gifts of all in our congregation and was the least important. Her big red hands, however, were gifts of the Holy Spirit and were used to cook hundreds and hundreds of pots of homemade soup with vegetables from Margaret's garden. Margaret seemed to have a private communication system with every family in the church whenever there was death, illness or a problem. She would show up even before the minister or the undertaker or the doctor with her old handbag and lift out a mason jar with its funny little wire holder for the glass top, revealing chunks of meat, potatoes, beans, carrots and tomatoes floating in a thick broth.

A mason jar of homemade vegetable soup, a huge smile,

and a promise that prayers were being offered—this was all that Margaret Simpson could bring. In my youthful sophistication, this seemed such an insignificant gift.

After thirty-three years as a minister, I now realize that Margaret Simpson and her gifts were just as important as golden-tongued oratory from the pulpit or silver-throated notes from the choir loft or iron-clasped handshakes from the narthex or steely minded arguments in the classroom. I thank God for Margaret Simpson, for Margaret Simpson's soup, smile and sentiments. The Spirit gave that congregation a needed gift in the person of Margaret Simpson. In retrospect, we who were in that church during the Depression now realize that Margaret was as indispensable as the preacher, the doctor or the undertaker.

Unfortunately, however, we cannot quite shake off this notion that some gifts are more important than others, or that some persons have more gifts and some have less. This was the problem in the church at Corinth.

What a contentious crew of Christians they were at Corinth, trying to pull rank on one another in regard to their spiritual gifts. Those who sometimes spoke in tongues felt superior and smug, claiming they were the elite and belittling any who didn't go into an emotional state of ecstasy in worship. Those who didn't speak in tongues or have a bent for expressing themselves like the charismatic crowd felt they had been neglected in the apportionment of the Spirit's gifts. There seemed to be a hierarchy of gifts in the congregation at Corinth, just as I had imagined there was such a hierarchy in the congregation of my boyhood. At Corinth, speaking in tongues seemed to be the only gift that really counted. At my home congregation, preaching in the pulpit seemed to be the only gift that counted. The Margaret Simpsons simply didn't count because no one thought they had any gifts, or their type of gifts didn't really count for much.

The New Testament insists that each Christian has a gift—

a unique gift—given by the Spirit. You have been given a unique gift by the Spirit! No one has all of the gifts, but each person has some gift and each gift is indispensable.

"Now there are varieties of gifts, but the same Spirit ... varieties of service ... varieties of working.... To each is given the manifestation of the Spirit ..." (1 Corinthians 12:4–7).

Paul goes on to give a sample list of some of the gifts of the Spirit among the Christians in Corinth. No priority is given to speaking in tongues. In fact, it's eighth in the list of nine examples. No special importance is attached to those who have the gift of preaching, for if we understand that to be prophesying, it comes as number six in the order.

Don't feel guilty because you cannot preach or sing or teach or perform one of the more visible functions of Christ's ministry. Don't feel envious of those who do preach, sing, teach or have a gift of the Spirit you do not have.

If the Spirit has given you a particular gift, as He has, and it is a gift that others notice and comment upon appreciatively, don't feel superior.

With Jesus Christ, there is no hierarchy. Every Christian believer is listed in His *Who's Who*. Jesus Christ confers value on each disciple, and the Spirit provides a gift to each disciple to serve.

You may feel overshadowed by others. You may be relegated to playing second fiddle in society's symphony. You will almost certainly be outranked by others in many of the groups with which you must associate. You will even be forced to feel unimportant by others trying to flaunt their position over you. But the Savior's signals are not those of our society. Jesus says, in effect, "It doesn't matter what the culture or your company may say about your standing. Your status with Me is never second-class. You are cherished for who you are! Now use your gifts to bring My *shalom* to the world."

In the Olympics, sports figures are preoccupied with winning. Winning is often driven by vanity and the will to dominate. Occasionally, competitors infringe on the rules in order to go for the gold. Occasionally, however, a chivalrous gesture takes place that causes everyone to pause in wonder, as in the 1964 Winter Games at Innsbruck, Austria.

Eugenio Monti, the Italian bobsled champion, had successfully bobbed through all the heats, eliminating all rivals except one. His last descent had been particularly fast. Then the announcement was made that further competition in the event would have to stop because Monti's only remaining competitor—his most dangerous rival—had broken part of his bobsled and had no replacement part. Monti's fans cheered, confident their hero was assured of the gold medal.

Monti hurried to his own sled, removed the identical part that was broken on his rival's bob, and sent the part to his competitor. The opponent installed Monti's part, made a last descent—and took the Olympic medal.

Observers agreed that if medals had been awarded for sacrifice, Eugenio Monti would have carried them all away. Sometimes, the greatest victories appear to be defeats!

Those who sacrifice to be second fiddles have written the glorious story of our faith in their blood. They seem to live and die in obscurity, but what a debt we owe them!

Would Saul of Tarsus, staggering into Damascus after his blinding encounter with the risen Jesus, have been able to become Paul the missionary without a second fiddle named Ananias?

Ananias appears briefly on the stage in Acts when Saul arrives in the city where he was determined to exterminate all Christians. Ananias undoubtedly knew that his name was on Saul's list. Other believers shrank from associating with the brutal persecutor. Perhaps even Ananias had misgivings: Was Saul's blindness real? Was the report of Saul's vision of Jesus a trick? Ananias remembered Saul's reputation. He understood the risks of welcoming such an enemy. Nonetheless, Ananias welcomes Saul, taking him into his home and nursing him. He nurtures Saul in the faith, then helps Saul escape from Damascus.

Saul the persecutor, who became Paul the apostle, won imperishable fame. Ananias fades into the background, completely overshadowed by the man he received and baptized.

You may be a second fiddle throughout your life—or even third or fourth. You may not be a Peter. You may not be a Paul. But you can be an Ananias.

In the words of the old hymn, you can sing joyfully and confidently:

> If you cannot preach like Peter,
> If you cannot pray like Paul,
> You can tell the love of Jesus,
> And say, "He died for all."

11

He Hears Our Unspoken Prayers

Some people don't pray. When they try to pray, they find praying comes hard.

Two men were fishing one Sunday morning. Their consciences began to bother them because they were not in church. Finally, one fisherman said, "You know, I feel a bit guilty that we're not in church this morning."

"Well," replied the other, "if it's bothering you, why don't you say a prayer or something?"

The first angler answered, "Okay. I'll say the Lord's Prayer."

"Oh, yeah? But you don't even know the words!"

"Want to bet I don't?"

"Sure do. Here's five bucks that you don't know the Lord's Prayer."

"Here's five bucks that I do!"

"You're on. Now let's hear it."

The first fisherman took a deep breath, closed his eyes and reverently intoned, "Now I lay me down . . ."

"Stop! Stop!" The second fisherman interrupted impatiently. "You don't have to finish. Here's my five. I didn't think you knew it!"

Some people don't pray because they have trouble praying.

Others, however, *won't* pray. They say they don't feel like praying. Sometimes, we don't feel religious. We may not sense God's presence. We cannot seem to muster much faith. We stop praying.

I sympathize with the characters in the story in which the woman of the house shouts upstairs one Sunday morning, "Come on, Johnny. Time to get up. It's Sunday morning, you've got to get dressed for Sunday school and church."

A sleepy voice answered, "Aw, but I don't feel like it. I'm still sleepy."

"Now get up at once. You're going to miss Sunday school and be late for church."

"But I'm tired. I don't want to go. Besides, it's boring."

The woman marched firmly upstairs. "Now look, John! You're thirty-seven years old and the minister of this church, and you've got to get up!"

Prayer also comes hard for those who *can't* pray for good reasons. There once was a little boy. He was seven years old and entering the second grade. He was new to his classmates and new to the school. He found they had all attended kindergarten and first grade together at that school, and he was the outsider. He felt alone. He wanted a dog. He prayed for a dog. He asked his mother and daddy for a dog. But those were Depression days in 1933, and money could better be spent on things other than dogs.

Finally, however, his father relented and went to the city pound and came home with a scruffy nondescript dog with faint spaniel ancestry. Never mind that the dog contracted distemper and had to be nursed through a long illness, and never mind that it shed dog hair at a prodigious rate on rugs and chairs, forcing it to be banished from the living room. To that little boy, the dog was his best friend. He called the dog simply Pal. He could hardly wait to get home from school to play with Pal, to walk with Pal, to talk to Pal. The boy prized Pal as his greatest blessing and remembered Pal in his nightly prayers.

One noon, the boy came home from school for lunch. His mother and father were waiting. The boy sensed something was wrong. Before they could say anything, he asked, "Where's Pal?"

His father's voice was husky. "Well, son, Pal ran out in front of a car this morning and got hit. We tried to do what we could for him, but he died."

Pal *dead?* The boy was devastated. He crouched on the back steps of the old kitchen and broke into uncontrollable sobs. His father and mother tried to comfort him, but all he could think about was his loss. Pal was dead. The boy finally ate some lunch and tried to choke back the tears as he was pushed out the door to return to school. He wanted to tell Miss Calhoun, the second grade teacher, but was too shy and kept the loss to himself. He cried again when he came home after school and didn't find Pal bounding up to meet him.

That night, when his mother asked him to say his prayers, the boy couldn't. "My dog is dead. Pal is dead," he whispered.

A few days later, sitting beside his mother at church, he heard the hymns and the prayers and the Scripture, but all he could think was, "Pal is dead. My dog is gone." The boy

could not say any prayers or sing any songs, but sat stoically
in loneliness and grief.

I once knew that little boy. His name was Bill Barker. And
that little boy later had times as a grown-up when events
sometimes made praying come hard.

The Spirit Helps Us

We may not know how to word our prayers. We may find
ourselves too weakened by grief or depression or failure to
verbalize a prayer. But the promise of the Lord is that He
takes even these glances and groans toward Him and makes
them into effective pleas for help and mercy.

> Likewise the Spirit helps us in our weakness; for we do not
> know how to pray as we ought, but the Spirit himself inter-
> cedes for us with sighs too deep for words. And he who
> searches the hearts of men knows what is the mind of the
> Spirit, because the Spirit intercedes for the saints according
> to the will of God.
>
> Romans 8:26, 27

Karen is a single parent. She carries the financial burden of
the family and finds that the paychecks barely cover the ex-
penses. There will be no vacation trip this summer for Karen
and the kids. Karen has grown weary of the loneliness and the
stress. Her job has no challenge, and advancement opportuni-
ties are nil. She still feels the pain of her divorce. Karen
pastes on her prettiest smile every Sunday and attends worship, but secretly she admits she is not very spiritual. Praying
comes hard for Karen. "Life seems to grind me down, and I
just can't seem to pray," Karen once confessed to two church
friends.

Tom is a sales engineer. Most of his working week seems to
be spent trying to make connections on flights to distant
cities. Strikes and weather snarl schedules. High interest rates
and a tight money market hinder sales. He tries to cope with

the pressures of a job demanding travel. Tom also tries to deal with the nagging sense of being an absentee husband and father to his own family. Tempting though it is to lounge on Sundays in the family room with the sports section and his coffee mug, Tom shaves and puts on his three-piece business uniform to attend worship with his family. However, he discovers that he is planning the calendar for the following week during the prayers and sermon. Praying comes hard. "I guess I'm too tired and busy to have meaningful prayers," Tom acknowledged to his wife.

Even if you don't fit the profile of either of these two persons, you can probably relate to them to some degree, because you also may find praying comes hard. It's not that you are consciously turning your back on the Christian faith. It's not that you are deliberately rejecting Christian living. It's not that you're going through any terrible "dark night of the soul." It's more the old story of what experienced Christians call dry spells. Except your dry spell seems more like a longer than usual trek across the desert. As one weary pilgrim put it, "The oases have seemed farther and farther apart recently, and I've drained my canteen this past week."

Take heart, for even the Apostle Paul and the New Testament Christians were not on a religious high every day. In fact, they had their spiritual dry spells. This is the point of the section from Romans 8 where Paul discusses the presence of the Spirit because of the Resurrection of Jesus Christ: "Likewise the Spirit helps us in our weakness; for we do not know how to pray as we ought, but the Spirit himself intercedes for us . . ." (Romans 8:26).

You may not feel like praying. You may not sense God is real. But don't despair. Jesus is praying with you. Jesus is praying for you. Jesus is praying in you.

And the Spirit "helps" us, as the translations put it. The Greek word used is powerful. With two prefixes making it an exceptionally positive verb, it means literally "to take hold of

at the side so as to support." The other place this word is used
in the New Testament is in Luke 10:40 where Martha, whin-
ing because she's been left to do all the work of meal prepara-
tion, demands, "Tell her [Mary] to *help* me."

The Spirit takes hold at your side to support you when you
may not be able to pray, but can only sob or groan as you
turn toward God.

Recently, I heard about a therapeutic procedure which
many of you are already familiar with, called patterning.
Some infants are born with a certain kind of brain damage
that keeps them from making the usual progress in devel-
oping skills such as crawling and walking. Basically, patterning means that nurses, attendants, parents, aides or whoever
take turns moving the infant's legs and arms in the pattern of
crawling. This procedure seems to help establish the pattern
of movement so that after weeks, or even months, the child
learns to crawl on his own.

The assurance of the Spirit is that He practices a type of
patterning with us. He patiently and tenderly works with us.
He takes even those cries and groans, those sighs and moans,
and He moves us into praying again. He makes us whole
again.

God shares. And God hears. The Lord knows what lies so
deep in your heart that you may not even be able to pray
about it in words. He decodes, sorting out your thoughts. He
untangles your random whims and fears and evasions and
needs. He translates the unarticulated, jumbled groans and
cries that are not anything resembling praying, yet are where
you are in your hurting and loneliness. "He who searches the
hearts of men knows what is the mind of the Spirit . . ."
(Romans 8:27).

The Spirit not only prays in you and with you and for you;
He also perseveres for you and with you and in you. "We
know that in everything God works for good with those who
love Him, who are called according to his purpose" (Romans

8:28). The Lord pulls all things together for good for those who care about Him and realize they belong to Him.

One December in Pittsburgh, I attended a Christmas party for handicapped children in a hospital. Fred Rogers, television's beloved Mister Rogers, and his pianist, Johnny Costa, were entertaining the children. One little boy, suffering from cerebral palsy, asked to sing a carol. The child's speech was halting and uncertain. When he began to sing "Silent Night," the sound was wavering and halting. The boy not only had difficulty in framing the words for the carol, but he shifted key on every note. As he meandered through the carol, the discordant sounds he labored so hard to produce were painful to hear.

Johnny Costa, however, quietly began to provide background music for the little boy's solo. On the portable organ, Costa wove beautiful chords with each note the child sang, and no matter how off key the line was, brought beauty and harmony into that child's singing. Costa seemed to anticipate where the little boy's next sound would be on the scale and worked the boy's note into one of the loveliest performances of "Silent Night" I have ever heard. In the same way, the Spirit takes and hears our prayers and perseveres with us.

The Greek word for *praying* means literally "to turn your attention toward God." The person who turns his or her attention toward God finds that God has been turning His attention toward him or her all the time! The Spirit is present, and always has been.

The Discipline of Prayer

There is an ancient story from the days of the desert fathers that describes a young man going out to the hut of an aged monk renowned for his depth of understanding into the ways of God. The young man, in a casual and somewhat flippant tone, said he wanted to know God. Would the old man show him?

The ancient saint said nothing but took the young seeker by the hand to a nearby stream. Leading him into the water, the old man grasped the young man firmly and pushed him under the water. Several seconds passed. With a fierce grip, the aged monk held the casual seeker under. The young man began to push, then to struggle. The old man continued to hold the other below the surface. The young man thrashed violently, then with a mighty heave, thrust himself above the water and inhaled great gasps of air. When his panting had subsided after a few minutes, he turned in bewilderment to the old monk.

The ancient sage, wise in the ways of the Lord and humans, finally spoke, quietly: "When you want God as deeply as you wanted air, only then will you find Him."

When you desire Christ as deeply as you desire food, you will find Him. When you acknowledge your dependence on Him, He becomes your companion on your pilgrimage.

"Ask, and it will be given you; seek, and you will find; knock, and it will be opened to you" (Matthew 7:7). These verbs in the Greek text are present imperatives, and the present imperative means to continue what you are already doing, or to keep on and on. *Ask and ask and ask; keep on and on seeking; persist in knocking.* "And it shall be given you . . . you will find. . . ."

We Protestants have been inclined to think of our prayer lives in terms of what has been traditionally known as devotions. Devotions are not mere psychological exercises. Nor are they therapeutic workouts. Prayer is not auto-suggestion; worship is not simply character building. Rather, prayer is the way whereby God, the creative One from whom we derive our being, comes to us. Prayer is the means by which the other reintroduces Himself.

Our Christian ancestors did not think or speak so much of *devotions* as they did of devotion. Like the wise old monk instructing the casual inquirer, these heroes and heroines in faith knew that devotion meant to persevere in praying as much as you persevere in breathing. They understood devotion to God called for relating to Him, not for what they got out of it, nor for a spiritual experience, but simply because to pray was to live. Unlike so many in our times who pray for a quickening pulse and a golden glow under the sternum, our fathers and mothers prayed unselfishly. They desired God for the sake of God! They sensed any other kind of prayer was a form of idolatry.

Even in our praying, we face the danger of idol worship. An idol, we remember, exerts a sinister fascination. Idolatry is when an idol becomes a perverted form of God. The idol usurps the place of God, becoming the formative center of our lives, drawing us away from being in the image of God and thwarting us from fulfilling the growth that the Creator has destined us to have.

One of the most insidious kinds of idolatry is thinking that we grasp God much as we master swinging a golf club or learn the tricks of bidding in playing bridge. We can easily fall into the idolatrous notion that we may possess God through praying.

We never possess God; God possesses us. We do not grasp God; God grasps us. God transcends all our human theologizing. He will not be owned; He refuses to be controlled. He allows us to know Him only when we let Him grasp and possess us.

Prayer is the process in which we learn to allow God to grasp us and possess us. A life of praying is the growth of a relationship with Christ as companion. Like any friendship, this relationship grows as a result of being in communication with each other.

The word *disciple* and the word *discipline* come from the same Greek word in the New Testament (*manthano*), which means "to learn by practice or experience." A disciple is a learner. Discipline is the way a disciple is formed. Learning is discipling and discipline.

Discipleship means being summoned to a discipline. If a

disciple is a learner, discipline is the training by which a disciple learns. And learning Jesus Christ and His way of sacrificial love is the hardest lesson of all. Training for this learning can only be done through a self-imposed discipline of daily praying.

There are no snappy shortcuts, especially when praying comes hard. Praying is not always easy, and sometimes seems filled with obstacles. Old habits reappear, luring us into self-indulgence. Busyness and pressures seem to distract us. Because God does not feel close, we begin to think that praying is too difficult. We give up on regular, systematic practices of praying.

Discipline in praying is essential. Without order and structure to our prayer lives, we simply will not grow in our relationship with Jesus Christ. There is no such thing as an "instant Christian" through the sudden emotional experience of answering an altar call or signing a decision card. Although an altar call or decision card may signify the start of a pilgrimage in faith as a result of Christ's call, we must undertake as rigorous a discipline in responding to that call as an athlete or soldier in training. In fact, the New Testament, especially in Paul's letters, consistently compares the Christian prayer life to the rigorous and regular workouts a crack athlete must undertake or the toughening exercises a member of an elite military unit must constantly practice.

The word *discipline* runs counter to what our culture preaches. "Express yourself! Do your own thing!" The emphasis has been on spontaneity. Pandering to the rebellious streak in each of us, some religious leaders have played down the place of a disciplined prayer life, saying that it is repressive and out of date.

In an age where trendy terms such as *freedom* and *liberation* signify no restraints and offer license for reckless self-expression, it may seem surprising to hear that discipline is actually liberating! When we adopt discipline in our praying,

we discover how creative praying becomes. Instead of re-
stricting us, the discipline frees us! Praying, instead of always
coming hard, becomes natural and essential.

You may ask, "How do you expect me as a busy person to
put structure and discipline into my prayer life?"

I reply, "How can you afford not to?" You *must* pray, even
when praying comes hard. Even when God seems absent.
Even when you try to convince yourself that you are too
busy. Even when you are hurting so much you cannot find
words for prayer. You must pray!

The risen, living Lord has already turned His attention toward you. In response, turn toward Him. In spite of your
doubts and feelings, continue to position yourself in His presence. You may want to shake your fist and scream at God
through clenched teeth. You may be inarticulate with grief.
You may feel no sense of spiritual stirring, no emotional
quickening. But persist in turning toward God, even when
your praying seems impossibly difficult and pointless.

You will discover that the risen One, through whom God
has already turned His attention toward you, takes your unspoken prayers and hears your deepest longings.

12

Jesus Understands Our Grief

Franklin Pierce seemed well equipped for the responsibilities of the presidency of the United States: He was well educated, he spoke effectively, had a commanding appearance, exuded charm and he was honest. His piety extended to his daily living. Everyone predicted he would perform brilliantly when he took office. Few, however, have failed more dismally.

Eight weeks before his inauguration, Franklin and Jane Pierce and their one living child, Benny, were traveling by train when the carelessness of a drunken brakeman caused an accident. The parents were only slightly injured, but Benny was caught in the wreckage and died. Ironically, the president-elect's son was the only fatality of the accident. Jane and Franklin Pierce were devastated with grief.

When the Pierces arrived in Washington a few weeks later, they asked that the usual inaugural festivities not be held. Mrs. Pierce continued to wear black mourning clothes for the entire four years her husband held office. Franklin Pierce also seemed to continue to live under a cloud of bereavement. He began to drink heavily to try to numb the feelings of grief over Benny's death. His presidency suffered.

Rejected for a second term because he was so ineffective, Pierce and his wife left the White House to return to New Hampshire after four miserable years in Washington. Their life in Concord, New Hampshire, continued to be unhappy. Although they attended worship each Sunday and held family prayers every day, they remained stupified by their sense of loss over their son. Unpopular even in his hometown, Franklin Pierce died in political and social obscurity. The death of their son was such an offense to the Pierces that they wallowed helplessly in grief.

Death always seems to be an offense. The finality of death, especially the death of a loved one, seems unacceptable.

We have bromides to try to offset the shock a loved one's death produces. We speak of "passing on." The hospitals state that one "expires," as if the word *dies* is obscene. We fondle platitudes about immortality. We search out reports of persons describing what it was like to have been resuscitated after heart failure and buy books purporting to be Baedeckers of the beyond. Hearses have become funeral coaches. Graves are now called burial estates. Funeral wreaths are known as floral offerings. Funeral directors are referred to as grief counselors.

Try as we may to be artful dodgers when it comes to death and dying, we keep remembering the one who died—and we mourn. The old adage "Time heals all wounds" does not always apply. The death of someone you love brings feelings that you cannot talk about easily. You are beyond the area of words.

Jesus knew this. When His friend Lazarus died, Jesus cried. He could not do otherwise.

The Greek word translated as "Jesus wept" in John 11:35 means literally that Jesus was wracked with sobs and had tears streaming down His cheeks. Jesus felt powerful emotions over losing Lazarus. He had feelings of hurt and regret, of concern and loneliness. Jesus also ached for the sisters, Mary and Martha. He knew what a desperate time they would face because of losing the family breadwinner. The Lord also realized that He would soon have to walk that lonely valley of the shadow. The awful and terrible finality of the grave faced Him as well as Lazarus. Death had presented itself in all its offensiveness.

Jesus wept. He had feelings. He did not try to hold back the tears. Through the person of Jesus, God has shown us that He has experienced the depths of human hurt.

Elisabeth Kübler-Ross, the famous author of *On Death and Dying,* once stated that all hospital chapels should be converted into "Screaming Rooms." She realized that there are times when we want to shriek with rage, especially when someone whom we love deeply dies.

Losing a loved one frequently fills us with anger. Where is God? Doesn't He understand? Doesn't God care? God is the hook on which we hang blame. Sometimes, we accuse God of punishing us. We denounce Him.

In case you think that it is unbiblical to express anger and bitterness, read some of the Psalms. They are blunt and gutsy. They show despair: "Out of the depths I cry to thee, O Lord!" (Psalms 130:1). They reveal doubts: "My God, my God, why hast thou forsaken me?" (Psalms 22:1).

But God can take it! He knows. He hears. He suffers. Through Jesus Christ, God assures us that He understands our grief. God has shown that He can deal with any offense, even death. Our God reached down into the nothingness of the grave after the crucifixion and bestowed new life. Through the Resurrection of Jesus Christ, God states that He can and will effect new beginnings for those who trust Him.

The promise of God is embodied in the person of Jesus. That promise is spelled out in the life, death and Resurrection of Jesus Christ.

This Jesus announces to two tearful, angry sisters grieving over the untimely death of their brother, Lazarus of Bethany, "I am the resurrection and the life . . ." (John 11:25).

It is as if Jesus is saying: "Through Me, you may know that you may depend on God to keep your loved one. I bestow life. I confer new life. I personally am here with you to counteract the destructive effects of death. I personally nullify the finality of death. Through Me, you have a peek through the veil to behold the mercy and power of God. I have the last word, not the coroner!"

These words of Jesus are not stained-glass rhetoric. God vindicated Jesus. He raised Him up from death. Through the Holy Spirit, the risen, living Lord continues to introduce Himself to us.

We have the vantage point of Easter. We are able to look at death differently. We know we may weep. We may even shake our fist at God. We can allow all our human feelings to spill out. We may shed our tears and sob our requiems, but we also realize that Jesus lives. He is the Resurrection, He is the life. ". . . because I live, you will live also," He announces to us (John 14:19).

After Jesus died on the cross, two people trudged out of Jerusalem. No "Hallelujah Chorus" was ringing in their ears, no miraculous signs were dazzling these two with an awareness of Jesus. In fact, this pair was not really expecting to have any sense of the Lord in their midst. All they could think of was how desolate they felt. Their closest friend was dead.

They did not realize that Jesus was there with them on that walk until later. It was only as they looked back on it that

they understood they were not alone and became aware that
it was not they who had let Jesus into their lives; rather, it
was He who let them come into His life.

For many, the sense of the Savior comes gradually. Like a
sunrise on a bleak wintry morning when the sun does not
come into view, but there is nonetheless the light of a new
dawn, the risen Lord approaches. God often approaches us
quietly and imperceptibly. The Comforter makes Himself
known gently and unexpectedly.

How often this has been the case in my life! At the time, I
was not really conscious of any cathedrallike sense of the
presence of the Lord. It was only in retrospect that I began to
understand that Jesus Christ was walking with me.

The telephone bell shatters sleep. I awake with a jerk. Pre-
dawn calls to a minister almost always mean bad news. I
fumble for the bedside light and note that the clock reads
5:00 A.M. It is Sunday morning, and as I try to shake sleep out
of my head I remember that I'm due to be at my church in a
few hours. As I reach for the receiver, wondering what the
emergency is, I privately wonder whether I'll be able to field
the crisis situation and get to the church on time.

"Hello," I rasp. My voice sounds thick.

"Bill?" a woman's voice says.

"Yes?" I reply, clearing my throat.

"It's Mother. I . . . I'm calling about Dad. He doesn't respond."

Suddenly, I am fully awake. It is as if I had touched an
electric socket. I recognize the voice of my mother-in-law. I
realize that she is talking about my wife's father.

She tells me the details. She has just heard him groan and
she cannot rouse him.

"Call the police emergency number. Immediately," I in-
struct. "And I'll come right over."

Trembling, I try to reassure my wife, who is now awake,
that she must not worry. "Probably a slight heart attack or

maybe a little stroke," I announce confidently. "I'm sure he'll be okay. After all, he's only sixty-one."

I drive through empty streets to the other side of the city, to the home of my in-laws. I feel a surge of confidence when I see the emergency van parked outside. Upstairs, I find the medics working on the limp form. I stand with my mother-in-law.

The minutes stretch into quarter hours. We note that the medics are not getting any response. The police doctor arrives. We watch him bend over the inert form of the man we love, listening intently with a stethoscope. Finally, the doctor stands up and turns to face us. "I'm sorry, but it's all over," he announces.

All over? At age sixty-one? But we need him! He's a husband . . . a father . . . a grandfather. So many people love him and want him alive!

All over, when there is so much he had planned to do? What about that trip to Europe that he and Jean's mother were counting on making? How they deserved it. After all those years of not having any money for frills, they had finally saved enough for their first big trip. I remembered some of the sacrifices that Jean's dad and mother had made for others. I recalled their dreams of retirement years on Cape Cod. And now . . . "all over."

God was certainly not in my thinking that morning.

Mechanically, I helped Jean's mother make a few of the necessary arrangements with the funeral director and called to break the news to the members of the immediate family. Then I drove back to the other side of Pittsburgh, shaved, changed into preaching garb and rushed to church to preach and conduct the 9:30 service.

My sermon sounded clumsy and labored to me as I struggled to put the words together. My prayers felt like hollow phrases. The Sunday church class I had to teach and the second service were even emptier and more mechanical. Periodically, I would grind to a halt, search for the next phrase and try not to repeat the police crew's comment, "All over. Sorry."

No one in the congregation knew at the time of Jean's dad's death, but some remarked afterward how helpful the service was. And the following week was no easier. There was the pressure of planning the funeral and handling necessary affairs. The funeral itself was positive and uplifting, but there was no particular consciousness of Jesus.

It was only as we looked back on those days of pain and loneliness that we began to understand that Jesus was with us, and we did not recognize Him in our midst. He did not give us dramatic signs. He did not offer us explanations of why a good man who was needed and appreciated should suffer a fatal coronary. But He quietly walked with us, we now realize. He was there with us in our lives, all the time. Although we did not experience any emotional jag or receive a spiritual charge, His gentle, healing presence steadied us.

I now know that the Lord is sometimes closest when I am least aware of Him. God is often nearest when we sense Him the least. When our powers are low, His power can most readily help us.

This was the experience of the two on the road to Emmaus that day after the reports of Resurrection. They had an unexpected Easter! He was present with them in spite of their inability to recognize Him in their company.

They could look back on the weary walk as one in which Jesus Christ was alive and present all the time because of that glimpse they caught of His reality as they broke bread together with Him. He had spoken to them earlier through Scripture, but through the table fellowship they knew it was the Lord.

This is why weekly worship is a necessity for us when we lose a loved one. It is not an option; it is not an extra; it is a *must*. For here in our midst, in the midst of the routine of singing praises together, praying together, listening to His story together, breaking bread and sharing the cup together in His name, He offers us assurance that He truly has been in our midst. He promises us that He lets Himself into our lives, even when we may not think we are letting Him in.

Tell Them What You Know

What about the time after Easter for you? What effect has the Resurrection had on your life?

For the earliest Christians, it meant a startling turnabout. From being timid, uncertain and embarrassed about their relationship with Jesus, they boldly went public with the news! Look at Peter. He was so hesitant a believer before the Resurrection that he would not even admit to being associated with Jesus. After meeting the risen Lord and realizing that He lived, Peter strode so straight and tall as a member of the Resurrection community that people brought their sick friends and relatives so his shadow would fall on them for healing! Peter and all of those early believers were so aware of the presence of the risen Lord that they went public with their faith and attracted others to the community of the faith.

What does the Resurrection mean to you? What effect has the risen Lord had on you? Are others aware that you are one of the Easter people?

Ralph Waldo Emerson lost his son, Waldo, and was devastated by grief. He turned to others for comfort and guidance. To his disappointment, all he heard were the commonplace banalities. Acknowledging his awareness of these, the great philosopher sighed that as soon as he pressed them for first-hand knowledge of the Lord, "They begin to quote." Turning to friends one day, Emerson asked them not to refer to the authors or the teachings, and added, "Tell me what *you* know."

"Tell me what *you* know," people around you are whispering or shouting. "Tell us what you know about the living Lord. Tell us what you know about the hope and promise of the risen One."

Wilma Voth married her husband, Carl, after her second year of college. She helped put Carl through college and Princeton Theological Seminary. When Carl was ordained and undertook pastoral responsibilities, Wilma worked closely with him. Together, they enjoyed a useful life. Carl's death came as a jolt. Only fifty-four, he had always been strong and active. Cancer took him in five months.

Wilma cried a great deal at first. Part of her weeping was for herself, because she knew she'd have to move out of the house belonging to the church. She didn't know where to go or how to plan the future. The unresolved feelings of grief, anger, fear, guilt and depression brought her suffering.

Wilma Voth, daughter of Mennonite wheat-farming people in Kansas, discovered for herself that Jesus Christ brings hope and healing. She returned to school, received her degree nearly thirty-three years after leaving college, then went on to take a master's degree in social work. Later, working with cancer patients and their families in the Vassar Brothers Hospital in Poughkeepsie, New York, Wilma Voth saw an opportunity to minister in Christ's name. Remembering her own hurt and anxiety as a widow and also realizing the maturity Christ brings, she organized a widows' support group. She searched the hospital's medical records for the previous two years and located women who had lost their husbands. From that first widows' mutual support group, three others have been established.

Christ guides us to ways of handling the worst of our problems, even the loss of loved ones, as Mrs. Voth learned in person! He is still the Resurrection and the life!

Let this risen Lord make you an instrument of new life for others.

13

He Resurrects Us
From Every Anxiety

William Clay Sargent was the vice-president of a prominent Wall Street firm and a member of the Stock Exchange. At thirty-five years of age, this financier seemed to be the epitome of success and the embodiment of the American dream. However, he resigned his positions. Why? Worry. He explained the anxiety leading him to leave Wall Street as a "fine, cold steel ball of fear that starts under your breastbone until you feel the chill of it in the marrow of your being. Strong drink covers it, makes you sleep, until the edge of night snaps and it is dawn again. Dawn again, and the Fear."

In spite of goods and titles, drinking and playing, anxiety produced "broker's disease"—a severe ulcer—in Sargent.

Anxiety: the cold steel ball of fear. The root of the English word *anxious* comes from the word for choking, obstruction, distress, pain. It dosn't take much imagination to notice the tie between the choking of the cold steel ball of fear under your breastbone and heart disease or broker's disease.

Americans drank 426.1 million gallons of liquor, 542.1 million gallons of wine, and 5.66 billion gallons of beer in 1984. Studies reveal that a frighteningly large percentage of this ocean of alcohol was consumed to ease the weight of the cold steel ball of worry.

Some sociologists and psychologists like to give each decade a title that succinctly describes the period. The Sizzling Sixties, for example, sums up the era of burnings in the black ghettos and assassinations of John F. Kennedy, Martin Luther King, Jr., and Bobby Kennedy. The Cynical Seventies portrays the disillusionment as the Vietnam war ground on and the Watergate cover-up was disclosed. This decade? The Anxious Eighties reflects the sense of dis-ease and worry plaguing most people during this decade of the late twentieth century.

In spite of euphoric announcements by some futurologists that scientific technology would bring in near utopia or that humans would conjure up brilliant new ways to solve all problems, we are worried people.

Sometimes the choking feelings of the cold steel ball result from fears that are purely imaginary. Sarah Perkins, for example, described her worries as a prisoner in Communist China. She spent over a year and a half in solitary confinement in a small cell. Every time she peeked out through the keyhole of the cell door, she observed an eye looking at her. Miss Perkins, although a Christian, found it unnerving to be scrutinized constantly and began to feel anxious about being observed all the time. After some time, however, she discovered that the eye at the keyhole was not human, but an artificial eye wired in place by her Communist tormentors. Sometimes fears have no more basis in reality than the eye at the door of Sarah Perkins's cell.

Real or imaginary, however, the cold steel ball chokes and presses. Swiss psychotherapist Carl Jung insisted that three-fourths of our energies that should go to fruitful outer work are locked up in interior conflicts because of anxiety.

And it's no go if we try to tell ourselves to ignore our fears and pretend they don't exist. We could well remind ourselves of the story of the little boy running down the street who was stopped by an elderly lady. "Where are you going so fast, sonny?" she asked.

"I'm running for a doctor. My grandpa is sick."

"Now you just run right back to your grandpa and tell him that he only thinks he's sick."

A few days later, seeing the same boy, the lady asked, "Tell me, how's your grandpa now?"

"Well, he's all right now. He thinks he's dead, and we're going to bury him tomorrow!"

Our worries cannot be talked out of existence.

The cold steel ball comes from many causes. Humorist James Thurber used to say that his boss, Harold Ross of the *New Yorker* magazine, lived at the corner of Work and Worry. Your anxieties may be job related. You may worry that your position may be abolished, or your department reorganized, or your group merged. Studies show that corporation executives are as tremblingly apprehensive about their jobs as factory workers suspecting they may be automated out of work. You do not realize how many others get off the bus on Friday evening not knowing for sure that there will be a desk for them in town on Monday.

Perhaps anxiety is a lot of cold steel balls under your sternum: money worries, health worries, future worries. We are anxious because we think we're not smart enough, not talented enough, not clever enough. We are anxious because we are helpless. We are anxious because we are failures, or are afraid we will be.

A basic American article of faith says that any individual can accomplish anything, if he only tries hard enough. While this is one of the glories of our free society, it is also a deep cause of anxiety. This notion encourages the old to try to grow young, the indecisive to try to become leaders, the dull to try to become intellectuals, housewives to try to become glamor girls, glamor girls to try to become actresses, and actresses to try to become novelists.

Try as we may, we will never manage everything satisfactorily. We will never find everything predictable. We will never guard ourselves completely against failure. We will never protect ourselves in absolute security.

We try to counteract our feelings of anxiety by wrapping some sort of security blanket around ourselves. With some it is what is in the bank, or a hefty, high-yield investment portfolio, or a string of properties, or expensive trinkets. A man I know had eleven restored foreign sports cars in a rented barn and boasted that his collection of antique autos was the best hedge against inflation—until the barn burned one night, destroying his toys.

Others attempt to deaden the fear inside by turning to the authority of power. Have you ever met someone who tries to control others, control events and control all contingencies? The most anxious person I have known was a woman who was so determined to restrain and influence her son that she selected his career (pastor of a church), his college and seminary, his congregations. She has never permitted him to marry, but has moved into the manses of each of his parishes to take charge. Needless to say, she has made this poor man most miserable. She denies that her worries are actually projections of her own inner confusion.

How many folks do you know who make death *the* most feared thing in their lives? Anxiety over what may happen to their bodies leads some to quack diets and eccentric health practices. But our security blankets will never be secure enough. They will all fail.

The Fear Within

No matter how much security you try to have, you cannot banish the cold steel ball. Some insist that the cold steel ball weighs the most when you are alone late at night. One person has dubbed these "the midnight futility fears." This type of worry provokes the free-floating anxiety of such questions as: Does what I do make any difference? Who would truly miss me if I died tonight? Is the world any better off because of what I'm doing? What eventually is going to happen to me?

These midnight futility fears bring to mind the ancient German myth of the huge snake, the Midgard serpent, which encircled the world, trying to crush everyone in its hideous coils. Sometimes the anxiety symptoms that squeeze your head and tighten your abdomen during a sleepless period are worse than the ghastly myth.

You want to find a place where you will be free from worry. Isn't there some utopia where the cold steel ball won't press on you so hard?

In northern Greece, on a steep rocky promontory jutting into the sea, surrounded by near-vertical cliffs, stands Mt. Athos. Mt. Athos is situated in a remote area and is almost inaccessible when you finally manage to find it. On the most precipitous pinnacle, a group of monks somehow managed to build a monastery centuries ago. The only way to get to this isolated spot is to be hoisted up the side of the cliff in a basket, and even this entrance can be made only when the sea is calm. Many have perished after slipping on the rocks and plunging into the surf below.

It is hard to find a place more cut off from the world than this monastery on Mt. Athos. The monks who live there are convinced that residing in that location frees them from the cold-steel-ball worries afflicting the rest of society. An American who joined their monastic community agreed. "I have none of the anxieties which nearly every other American has," he stated. "But," he added, "I have to admit that I worry sometimes whether I did the right thing to come to this place. And I sometimes worry whether coming here will truly bring me salvation."

After fleeing Wall Street, William Sargent thought he'd buy a camper and spend some time drifting around the country. However, he admits, "The fear still lurks within."

Exactly.

Jesus never suggested that anyone withdraw from the world. He did not advocate moving to a monastery on Mt. Athos or living as a roving recluse in a camper. In fact, Jesus never pulled people away from the struggles and tensions that made up their lives.

Instead, Jesus told people to shift the center of gravity of their lives, to relocate the focus of their attention. He never mentioned anything about changing activities. Not a word about a change of location. Rather, He insisted on a change of heart.

The problem, Jesus knew, lay within a person, not without. He knew that the fear would still lurk within.

We prefer not to think about what lurks within. A high school teacher in a small town in Missouri taught a course in physiology. One day, the teacher received an angry letter from a parent of one of the members of his class. The note concluded, "I don't want my Alice to learn no more about her insides."

We sometimes do not like to face what we are. But because He cares about us, the Lord makes us see what's really inside our hearts and minds. Only then may we receive His grace. Only then may we be healed. Only then will we grow! When we look within, we will learn to cope with the cold steel ball.

What lurks within most of us is turmoil. "I am a walking civil war," reports a worried salesperson.

"Fear Not"

Fear is being in awe of some authority. Worry is respect for power, money, death, prestige, or whatever. Anxiety is being focused on the wrong authority or power.

Currently, you are focusing on the page of this book. You may be aware that there is a lamp and a table beside you. You may also be conscious of having hands to hold the book, and you may know there is a dog and a radio nearby. But you are not preoccupied with the lamp or the table, your hands, the dog or the radio. You manage to separate what is marginal from what is focal. When God's rule has central concern in your life, you are not focusing on marginal matters. You have them in the proper perspective.

As a Christian, you focus on Jesus. You have a sense of awe toward Him. You recognize that Jesus Christ is the authority in your life. You have a deeper respect for Jesus than for any other power.

The words of the psalmist speak of a "clean" fear: "the fear of the Lord is clean, enduring for ever . . ." (Psalms 19:9). This is awe and respect toward the Lord. This type of fear, which the Bible describes as clean, can cleanse you. All other fears should be labeled dirty fears. Fear or awe of anything or anyone except God will disrupt your life and eventually destroy you. But the fear of the Lord, the cleansing fear, lifts you from the worries that press like the cold steel ball.

Throughout Scripture, the oppostite of faith is not doubt, but fear. Faith is focusing on the Lord. Fear, the opposite, is focusing on the lesser. This is why the New Testament states, ". . . perfect love casts out fear . . ." (1 John 4:18).

Focusing on the Lord means putting the other powers and authorities trying to awe you in their proper place. You owe them nothing! You don't worship them. The culture may, but you don't. You will remember that the earliest Christians, nonconformists because they refused to worry about those other gods (including the threat of the state putting on airs of deity), were denounced as atheists! You acknowledge God as sole Lord. You recognize that only He is to be taken seriously. You don't fret and worry over the claims of any other. You know that God knows you and your needs.

Jesus stated that the Lord even knows how many hairs you have on your head (*see* Matthew 10:30). If God knows this, He can be trusted to know all your needs. Even the hairs of your head are numbered. How incredible! How absurd it sounds! Max Factor of Hollywood once employed a girl to count the hairs on a woman's head. It was a tedious job, but the tally showed that on her head there were 135,168 hairs. On a man's beard there were 60,000 hairs; on a mustache, 7,000.

If God knows the count of every hair on every head, there can be no other to take His place. He is the Lord!

A New Testament scholar looked up the number of times the words *fear not* are found in the Scriptures. He was astonished to locate the phrase ninety-nine times! Add other words of Jesus, such as the number of times He said "Do not be anxious," which actually means, "don't worry!" and the number rises.

Martha's problem during her dinner party was that she had lost her perspective. She allowed herself to become awed by her responsibilities as a hostess. She lost her focus on Jesus, her guest. Jesus didn't criticize her for being in the kitchen. He knew that someone had to set the table and fix the food. When worrier Martha blew up at her sister for not being a fellow fusser, Jesus gently reminded the woman with the cold steel ball pressing so hard that she couldn't keep her composure, "Martha, Martha, you are anxious . . ." (Luke 10:41).

But Jesus also brought this anxiety-ridden woman His friendship. Even when Martha's life was so choked with wor-

ries over food and table settings and guest lists and posses-
sions and a dozen other distractions, Jesus did not give up on
her. He patiently sat with practicing idolater, Martha of
Bethany.

And Jesus promises that He continues to be with you, in
spite of the anxieties spoiling your relationship with Him.
You can say, "Thank You, Lord, for standing with me. You
accept me, riddled with anxieties. You promise that You will
be with me, worries and all. You offer me a new beginning
when I think the cold steel ball means a miserable ending."

The writers of the Bible also knew about the cold steel ball
of fear and the way it chokes. Their age was also an era of
anxiety. They were subject to the same worries that you
know.

But those who were fathers and mothers in faith also knew
the presence and power of the Lord in their lives. They knew
that the God who was strong enough to move aside a stone
slab of the garden tomb was also able to pull the cold steel
ball of fear from under their breastbones.

Take Paul. He had plenty to worry about. He was chained
to a Roman soldier day and night. He was uncertain what the
outcome of his imprisonment would be. When Rome closed
her claws around a man, she rarely let go until she drew
blood. Paul did not know what dangers lay ahead—torture, a
horrible form of execution, more years of prison because of
bureaucratic neglect, additional miscarriages of justice and
delays in trial. Paul understood how unpredictable Emperor
Nero could be, and he had firsthand experience with brutal
guards and jail-house goons.

Paul also remembered with anxiety the string of tiny,
struggling churches he had founded. He knew their desperate
needs and realized how helpless he was to help. Paul realized
that these faltering new believers were beset from without
and within. He worried that they wouldn't be able to stand
up to persecutors and hostile townspeople. He was anxious

that these recent converts not be swayed by troublemakers who insisted on a narrow-minded legalism or advocated a freewheeling permissivism. Paul was aware that enemies were trying to undermine his efforts and that many of his congregations were being torn apart by controversies. How does a person feel when he hears that the people he loves and the cause he has served are in jeopardy?

Paul does not write cheery messages. He doesn't pen pep talks. He doesn't play down the problems, the dangers. He does not call on his readers to show some kind of false courage, to try to draw on their own frail resources. Never, because Paul knew how the cold steel ball of fear quickly chokes off our puny strength.

Instead, Paul tells his anxiety-ridden friends, ". . . The Lord is at hand. Have no anxiety about anything . . ." (Philippians 4:5, 6). "The Lord is at hand!" Paul almost sings the words as he dictates to his friend who will carry the note back to Philippi. The Lord is at hand! Jesus Christ will ultimately triumph. The King is at the door! Through this Good News, God's Good News, Paul gives his anxious friends an antidote for anxiety.

Paul's correspondence is more than a set of letters to worriers. It is God's word to us today. The Good News for us is that the Lord is still at hand, and therefore the cold steel ball will not crush us. We no longer need to fret about failing. We need not worry about doing the right thing. We do not have to trouble ourselves over past inadequacies. We are freed from being anxious over whether we are successful or attractive or intelligent. We need not insist on having life predictable and manageable. We can be worry-free enough to take risks, make mistakes, pick ourselves up again, laugh, and start over.

Intuitively, we all know that every little security blanket will fail us and we will have to face the ultimate anxiety: "What will become of me?" Now we come to the root of all worry. We are up against the final dread. The real reason for our anxiety is thinking that we are rushing toward a state of nonbeing.

We know that beyond our brief time here on this planet are billions of years. After our fleeting appearance, we can foresee only silence and nothingness. We fear that we will be extinct and forgotten. We think we hear the tempter (who is a nihilist) whisper with a sneer, "There is no sense whatsoever in your life, no hint of meaning to human existence. And eventually, there will be no trace of you."

But God has already handled that fear for you! He has resolved that ultimate anxiety. God took the cross—the symbol of dread—and raised up the One condemned to be extinguished and forgotten on it. The Almighty turned a bleak, black weekend at Calvary, when the cold steel ball crushed Christ and everyone connected to His ministry, into the Resurrection celebration. God brought back Jesus as living, risen Lord.

God has taken care of the final anxiety for you. He has already answered your unspoken query, "What's going to happen to me?" He assures you that He can handle the future, including your personal future. The One who bestowed the gift of life on you promises that He continues the relationship with you. He remembers you because He values you! He resurrects you from every anxiety. He is at hand!

Alistair Maclean, the beloved pastor in a highland glen in a remote part of Invernesshire, once quoted a woman who summed up God's antidote for anxiety in a poetic way: "I know," she said, "the secret of happy living. 'Tis to sail the seas and ever to keep the heart in port."

You can endure any worry in life as long as you are centered on the One who conquered the threat of the cold steel ball under your breastbone!

14

Shovers and Seethers All

It happened in the Pittsburgh airport. I was waiting at the ticket counter to check in. The agent was obviously inexperienced and was preoccupied on the telephone. I was first in line, standing patiently while the ticket agent continued his exasperatingly long telephone conversation.

Finally the agent hung up the telephone. I picked up my briefcase, starting to move toward the counter. Suddenly a burly middle-aged figure in a dark suit and hat stepped up to the counter in front of me and handed the agent his ticket. His action was rude and aggressive. The agent, obviously not wanting to be caught in the middle of an unpleasant situation, pretended not to notice. A couple of passengers behind me grumbled menacingly. The man, who had cut into line without any apology to us or thank you to the agent, took his boarding card and turned around. It was then that I noticed his clerical collar.

I seethed with anger. It was bad enough he pushed into my place, but it made me more hostile when I realized he was a clergyman. Shoving me around like that! Who did he think he was, especially as he represented an ethic of love? Somebody ought to report that guy to his superiors!

Suddenly the conviction hit me. Here I was, also a clergyman, seething with hurt, annoyance and irritation over this individual who had violated my rights. Two clergymen— both guilty of lack of love! One a shover; the other a seether. Each of us represented the love ethic, each ostensibly was dedicated to serving and caring, each preached about love for years, each celebrated the sacrament of sacrificial mercy—and there we were, shoving and seething.

Shovers and seethers—that's who we are, priests and ministers included. Sometimes one, sometimes the other. No one here lives by love, in spite of the way we nod approvingly at 1 Corinthians 13.

Each of us is pricked and bruised each day with a series of snubs and hurts from others. We can quickly tally and catalogue an astonishingly large number of incidents in which others have offended us.

Novelist Thomas Hardy was married to a woman who literally kept score of her hurts. His wife, Emma, wrote all her many grievances against him in a notebook titled "What I Thought of My Husband." Hardy discovered the notebook as he was going through Emma's effects after her death and found it so appalling that he threw it into the fire.

We can nurse our hurts until they make us miserable. Andrew Jackson did this. During his campaign for president, opponents brought up rumors of scandal about his wife's divorce at the time of Jackson's marriage to her thirty-eight years earlier. Jackson was deeply hurt by the slander. Rachel, however, became distraught. Shortly after the election, she suffered a heart attack and died. Andrew Jackson let his hurt fester. Grief-stricken and resentful, President Jackson blamed his foes for her death the rest of his life. "May God Almighty forgive her murderers as I know she forgave them," he growled constantly, then always added, "I never can." And he did not forgive. Conflict roiled his eight years in office. He died a bitter man.

John F. Kennedy's friend Benjamin C. Bradlee wrote a best-seller, *Conversations With Kennedy,* in which he stated that the president lived by "that wonderful law of the Boston Irish political jungle: Don't get mad; get even." Bradlee's statement, however, applies not only to Kennedy and the Boston Irish and politicians. "Get even!" is the maxim by which most of us live.

An old man was celebrating his one hundredth birthday. "What are you most proud of?" he was asked.

"Well," said the man, "I've lived one hundred years and haven't an enemy in the world."

"What a beautiful thought. How truly inspirational," commented the reporter.

"Yep," added the centenarian, "outlived every last one of them."

This is about the best our culture can do about getting along with enemies. All right, so you don't retaliate—at least not openly—but you sure don't exert yourself in trying to re-establish a relationship with them. You ignore the so-and-so's.

Contrast this notion to Jesus, who says *"forgive!"* not "outlive."

Meanwhile, we try to be Christians. But we discover our religion becomes hollow when we think of getting even.

When Charles Peguy, the great French writer, published his masterpiece on Joan of Arc, critics cruelly panned both the poem and Peguy. Charles Peguy was deeply hurt and angry toward his critics. Retreating within himself, the sensitive poet could not bring himself to forgive his reviewers for their harsh words about him or his *Joan*. Much later, Peguy described his rage in a letter to a friend. "Would you believe it," he wrote, "that for eighteen months I could not say 'Our Father . . . Thy will be done'? It was quite impossible to say. I could not accept His will. It was even more impossible for me to pray, 'Forgive us. . . .' " The words, Charles Peguy reported, "would have stuck in my throat."

Without forgiving others, any requests for God's forgiveness seem to stick in our throats instead of reaching the Lord.

You have been hurt. You carry wounds from others. So do I. Maybe you have forgiven once or even a dozen times. But Jesus reminds you that you cannot carry those grudges. Perhaps you have told yourself that you will not try to retaliate, but at the same time you will not bother to extend yourself for others.

A young pastor came to see me several years ago. He recited a list of grievances he held against members of his congregation. His alleged hurts amounted to exactly the same ones we all experience, but this minister was sure that his were unique to him. When he paused finally, I suggested that perhaps part of his problem was his difficulty in forgiving people. He looked indignant. "What do you mean? I've forgiven them and forgiven them. How many times is a guy supposed to forgive a bunch like that?" Before I could reply, he launched into a new tack. It seemed he had fantasies of getting a fellowship or grant and studying for a graduate degree to teach philosophy.

I never did get to tell him of another friend, teaching in a philosophy department in a college, who had dropped by a few days previously. This friend had poured out his litany of hurts and snubs from faculty and administration. After telling me emphatically that he had forgiven these ingrates for the last time, he asked me how he could go about getting out of his faculty position and into serving in a pastorate!

How Often Must We Forgive?

We want to put limits on our forgiveness. "I'm tired of being trampled on. They've had too many breaks. How long am I supposed to be showing kindness and turning the other cheek? I've had it with this mercy stuff with *him*." We want to measure out our mercy.

Peter thought about the times he had been hurt by others and the extent of forgiveness. "Lord how often shall my brother sin against me and I forgive him? As many as seven times?"

Peter considers himself generous. He feels pleased with himself. He is truly doing far more than the rabbis taught ("Forgive three times but not the fourth") by showing twice as much mercy and then some. Peter expects Jesus to say, "Good for you, Peter. You couldn't possibly act more magnanimously than that!"

Instead, Jesus shakes His head. "I do not say to you seven times, but seventy times seven!" Jesus refuses to let you set limits to love. You cannot reduce faith to a mathematical equation. You cannot turn mercy into a measurable amount. You forgive, and forgive, and forgive—as He forgives you.

It is relatively easy to be kind toward people you like or who like you, or who appeal to your sympathy and arouse your pity. But it is hard to show mercy toward those who hurt deliberately. Here is where you employ your little calculators, contriving to show as little regard as you can get away with.

God does not keep score. God does not count cost. How many times does He act in mercy toward you? More than you can tally. More than you deserve. You are a bankrupt debtor with no assets before Him.

That is the significance of the cross and the Resurrection of Jesus. The grace of our Lord Jesus Christ communicates God's incredible mercy. Although we humans have repeatedly done the unspeakable against God, He forgives not just once, not twice, not even seven times, but countlessly. Although God could say, "I have had it with you; I have forgiven and forgiven at great cost to Myself," He has continued to be merciful.

Perhaps you have forgiven another once or twice, but find yourself remembering the injury. You might have forgiven, but you have not forgotten. You find yourself growing resentful and angry, even years later.

A man I know was considered for an important promotion at work. He was disappointed when another was brought in from outside for the position. The outsider treated the man who'd wanted the position with contempt. The newcomer made the man who'd been there in the first place so uncomfortable and made his working conditions so difficult that he finally left.

My friend struggled with his feelings of hurt. He prayed to act as a Christian. He confesses that it has not been easy to handle the resentment toward the man who forced him out. Although my friend says he forgave the other, he acknowledges that he has not forgotten the hurt. Periodically he remembers the pain he felt at the time he was displaced. In fact, he occasionally finds the outsider who gave him such a hard time asking for favors. "How many times must I forgive this guy who hurt me so deeply?" my friend wonders.

Love has no arithmetic.

The Model of Love

It was a dismal, familiar story of a man in his late forties on long business trips to the Orient who was unfaithful to his wife. Perhaps Jim was trying to justify himself, but he told Helen, his American wife, that he was tired of being married to her and was in love with Haruka, a pretty young Japanese girl. Jim divorced Helen after twenty-five years of marriage and moved out to be free. His company continued to send him to the Far East on business. He picked up the affair with the woman in Japan each time he visited Tokyo. When Haruka sent word that she was pregnant, Jim felt twinges of guilt and uneasiness. He cabled some money. During the next few years, Jim continued to visit Haruka and their baby daughter, Jasmine, and give them a small allowance.

Suddenly Jim was taken violently ill. The doctors examined him and discovered he had a rapidly spreading form of cancer. In spite of surgery and chemotherapy, Jim quickly grew weak and realized he would not live more than a few months. Friends told Helen, Jim's ex-wife. Helen had gone through all the stages of hurt and anger when Jim had left, but she still remembered that she was a Christian. One day, Helen appeared at Jim's bedside in the hospital. She and Jim tried to talk, but it was difficult. Finally Jim broke down and cried, asking for Helen's forgiveness. Helen groped for words. "Is there anything I can do?" she found herself asking.

"It's Haruka and Jasmine," Jim whispered. "I've used up nearly all my money on this sickness, and I don't know what will happen to them. All my insurance is being left to you."

Helen couldn't answer. She left Jim's hospital room and struggled in prayer for several days. A few days before Jim died, she wrote to Haruka and Jasmine, inviting them to come live with her. A month after the funeral, a moving scene took place as a fragile Japanese girl and frightened child were taken into the arms of Helen and welcomed as family. Helen has made a home for them and thanks God for the way she has learned to appreciate His undeserved mercy.

In your hurt, you need more than moralisms about being merciful. You need a model. Love as an abstraction is not enough; you need a living demonstration of forgiveness in the face of hurts.

Jesus is the model of love. The more I see of Him and try to learn about Him, the more I am confronted with the most complete and satisfactory model of God's love. In Jesus, I am introduced to the presence of God's love in life.

Jesus never cleared His throat and pompously announced, "Now I shall demonstrate an act of mercy. Lights, please." Instead, the Gospel accounts portray Him showing mercy day in and day out toward everyone He encountered.

When some Samaritan villagers treated Jesus and His friends rudely, refusing them hospitality one day, the incensed disciples demanded that He let them burn them down: "Call down fire!" (See Luke 9:51–56.) The disciples seethed over the Samaritans' hurt. Jesus dealt creatively with the anger of both the Samaritans and the disciples. His way of long-suffering love and forgiveness in the face of hurt is a model.

When Judas betrayed Jesus, Jesus graciously shared morsels He personally dipped with Judas—an act reserved for close associates. Even when Judas approached to identify Jesus for the police, Jesus greeted him as a friend. Jesus persisted in reaching out to try to salvage Judas, refusing to hate, continuing to care. He forgave. He is the model; He shows the presence of God's love in life.

When the execution squad carried out its horrible assignment, and when the crowd taunted and jeered, Jesus gasped, "Father, forgive them; for they know not what they do . . ." (Luke 23:34).

We need a model, but we also need motivation to love. Knowing is not enough. That motivation comes only when we first receive love. We are motivated only when the power of God's love is realized in our lives.

God has taken and accepted all our shoving and all our seething. He has accepted us. He has borne with us in love. The cross is God's way of stating that He accepts us in spite of our most unlovable characteristics. The love of Jesus Christ motivates you to care in the face of the deepest hurts by others.

Few have had to endure more hurts than Martin Luther King, Sr. A sharecropper's son, Daddy King, as he was affectionately known, experienced the snubs of racial prejudice

and suffered the barbs of racial hate. His life was marked by
personal hurts. In 1968, his son and namesake was assassi-
nated. In 1969, another son died in a drowning accident. In
1974, his wife of forty-eight years was shot by a gunman during a worship service in King's church. In spite of all the
hurts Daddy King had to take, however, he never gave way
to hate or bitterness. "Nothing a man does," he said, "takes
him lower than when he allows himself to fall so low as to
hate anyone."

How could Martin Luther King, Sr., go through eighty-
four years of hurts and speak like that? Simply because he
was motivated by the power and presence of the living Lord.
King had experienced God's grace.

Our Priestly Duty

God's mercy is indivisible. The inward flow of His goodness is impossible without an outward flow toward others.
Nothing separates you faster from God than a tough, unfor-
giving attitude toward another. Your bitterness and anger is
destructive of all relationships. Apart from the warmth of
God's presence and mercy, you gradually freeze, and as the
person freezing to death eventually sinks into torpor, the man
or woman who refuses to love is so separated from God that
he or she finally fails to notice the cold. You thaw only when
you take the kind of positive action that God takes toward
you.

This is why Jesus says, "Blessed are the merciful, for they
shall obtain mercy," and "Forgive us our sins as we forgive
those who sin against us."

Protestants take seriously the fact that everyone is a priest.
This means more than not having to go through ecclesiastical
organizational channels in order to reach a personal assurance of divine mercy. You, having received mercy from the
Lord, are intended to pronounce absolution on others. You
are to mediate forgiveness. You are to announce authorita-

tively that Jesus Christ brings acceptance to guilt-ridden people. Your priestly duties are to confer that new standing and provide new beginnings. You, too, absolve brothers and sisters.

Willie Stargell, of the Pittsburgh Pirates, is such a priest. In the tense days before the Pirates captured the 1979 National League pennant, Dale Berra dropped a fly ball in the ninth inning, costing his team the game. Berra sat by himself in front of his locker after the game, wracked with a sense of failure and paralyzed with guilt. He could not bring himself to join his teammates to eat or talk.

"Pops" Stargell, however, heaped up a plate of food, carried it over to young Berra and handed it to him. Laying his big hand on Berra's shoulder, Stargell said, "Now, Dale, you weren't the only one who lost the game; we all feel we lost it with you, and we are family."

A priestly act, anointing another with the ointment of mercy and doing a beautiful thing to a hurting, guilt-obsessed human.

Will you be such a priest? Will you commit yourself to bring healing and forgiveness to those you meet this week? No Christian can sleep at night without pronouncing absolution on everyone he has met that day or everyone he knows. The Jesus who shows you that there is a God who loves you enough to forgive sends you to release His power and healing to others!

15

Overcoming the Tomb of Guilt

A t the close of World War I, Emile Verhaeren wrote a book recounting his brutal experiences in the trenches during the bloody conflict. The book was dedicated, "To the Man I Used to Be."

This could also be the story of our lives. Or we could inscribe our individual biographies, "To the Person God Meant Me to Be."

We live with guilt.

Sometimes our sense of doing wrong comes from acts we have done, intentionally or unintentionally.

A soldier in Vietnam was on river patrol one evening. Taut

and tired from heat and strain, he nervously watched the shores. Suddenly, a cluster of figures appeared on the bank upstream. The soldier opened fire with his automatic weapon, then he and his buddies cautiously moved up to the place they had targeted. They discovered they had killed two women, three small children and a baby—all unarmed.

The feeling that we've done wrong obsesses us. With the guilt-stricken James Tyrone in Eugene O'Neill's *A Moon for the Misbegotten*, we can only cry, "No present, no future. Only the past happening over and over again."

Even the great Samuel Johnson, the pious and learned English writer, continued to reproach himself throughout his life when he remembered how in his boyish pride he had refused to look after his father's bookstall in the Utexeter market. Once, in an effort to ease the ache of that memory, Johnson, then in his seventies, went back to Utexeter and stood for hours in the rain with his head uncovered at the spot where the bookstall had been.

Sometimes our sense of knowing we have done wrong arises from what we have not done, or what the old prayer books used to call "sins of omission."

A woman had been caring for a husband afflicted with a serious heart problem. One afternoon, with his encouragement, she accepted an invitation to play bridge with some friends for a few hours. She left him comfortably resting in bed. When she returned two hours later, she found her husband's body. Although the doctor assured her the fatal coronary could not have been averted, the woman is convinced that if she had remained at home that afternoon, her husband would not have died.

After John Kennedy's assassination in Dallas in 1963, his widow, Jackie, continued to think that if only she had been looking to the right, she would have seen the first shot hit Jack. Then she could have pulled him down, thus saving him from the second shot. The memory of this failure obsessed the poor woman.

Sometimes we get a feeling we have done wrong through the guilt others lay on us.

Several years ago, Dan Greenberg wrote a humorous best-seller called *How to Be a Jewish Mother* in which he said you do not have to be either Jewish or a mother to master the techniques needed "to plant, cultivate and harvest guilt." Greenberg states that drill number one calls for presenting your son two shirts as a present. When the son wears one of them for the first time, you look at him sadly, and with a tone of deep hurt you sigh, "The other one you didn't like?" Everyone has been made to feel like that boy somewhere, someway, sometime.

A young couple I know have the notion that they have not done enough for their small children because they have not taken them to Walt Disney World. It seems most of the neighbors have trekked to Florida. They are barely squeezing by financially and the trip to Walt Disney World is impossible on their present income. So the husband has taken a moonlighting job in a gas station nights and weekends, and the mother is trying to find part-time work from midnight to morning. Their family time together has been reduced to almost nothing, but the guilt-induced sense of failure threatens their health and stability. Others have issued so many guilt-trip tickets that they feel compelled and driven. They will go to Walt Disney World not so much because they want to as because they feel guilty. Theirs is literally a guilt trip!

Sometimes we have a vague feeling that something is not right with ourselves. It's hard to put a finger on the reason, but we have a sneaky sense that it may have something to do with our faith.

Charles de Foucauld was a Frenchman who wasted the early part of his life as a drifter and soldier. Thrown out of the army, he spent most of his time in the slum bars of French-speaking North Africa. Meanwhile, he felt a restlessness. De

Foucauld returned to France. Always a nonbeliever, de Foucauld wandered into a Paris church one day. He told the priest, Abbé Huvelin, "I have not come to confessional; I have no faith."

The Abbé replied, "It is not your faith that is at fault, my friend, but your conscience."

Charles de Foucauld later confessed his sins and learned the experience of Christian forgiveness. He began a spiritual pilgrimage that led him to join the Trappist order of monks. He subsequently was sent to Algeria with the Little Brothers, where his service in the Sahara became legendary. Charles de Foucauld was killed during World War II, sharing the forgiving love of God, which he had learned personally brings hope for all sinners. His work continues in Algeria today, respected by Moslems and Christians alike.

Our consciences, not our faith, make us feel we have done wrong, or give us a sense of restlessness.

In the Middle Ages, some cunning sadist devised a type of dungeon called "Little Ease." Designed to torture a person by cramping him in a confined space, the cell was not high enough to let the victim stand up nor wide enough to lie down. The victim was forced to live a perpetual semisquatting position. Sleep was a collapse. The unchanging restriction stiffened the body. Unable to stand as a free person yet unable to slump as an animal, the helpless person in the "Little Ease" was reminded that innocence meant standing as a free person.

Knowing that you have done something wrong is like living in the "Little Ease." Whether your guilt comes from something you have done, something you have not done, or from feelings others have made you have, you sense something is not right with yourself.

Amazing Grace

Escape? How do you hammer down the walls of the dungeon of guilt feelings? Shucking off blame or trying to make amends will not cause the feelings of guilt to leave. We cannot rationalize guilt so that it will go away. Nor can we resolve the feelings by working harder to be good. We need someone to hammer down the walls of the dungeon. And this is what God has already done through Jesus Christ!

When people entombed Jesus Christ after murdering Him, in a sense they also entombed themselves. Peter, Judas, the soldiers, the jeering mob—everyone who had anything to do with the death of Jesus—was guilty. God could have chosen to let them all stay that way. After all, He might have reasoned, they had it coming to them. Served them right, agonizing in the isolation, failure and guilt. God could have decided to let them all remain that way permanently.

But God hammered aside the tomb of Jesus Christ. He raised Christ up from the dead. And in so doing, He hammered apart the tomb of guilt. God bludgeoned the prison of loneliness, fear, failure and guilt trapping Peter, the followers, the execution squad, the callous crowd, the smug Sanhedrin—even Judas! The mighty hammer of mercy smashed the guilt they all had to live with.

After the Resurrection, people remembered how Jesus had died. They recalled that He had looked down on the callous soldiers and bystanders and saw them for what they were. Yet they remembered that Jesus also saw them for what they were meant to be. "Father, forgive them, for they know not what they do," they recollected Jesus saying.

In spite of the cruelty at the cross, God shows mercy! God applied His hammer of love and broke down the walls of the dungeons of guilt for the earliest followers of Jesus.

The astounding news is that God continues to do so!

Have you understood that for yourself?

John Newton lived a life of hopeless degradation. He was a rough seaman who rose to command his own ship. He indulged in nearly every form of vice. For four years, he ran slaves from the African coast. Then he was confronted by the

Gospel and converted. He became a strong Christian, but he couldn't forget his sordid past. However, the future he had through Jesus Christ kept him from despair. He personally realized the meaning of God's mercy through Jesus Christ. Among Newton's accomplishments are several of our most loved hymns, including "How Sweet the Name of Jesus Sounds," "Glorious Things of Thee Are Spoken" and "Amazing Grace."

Over the mantel in his study, Newton fashioned a sign in large letters as a constant reminder of the meaning of that amazing grace: "Thou shalt remember that thou wast a bondsman in the land of Egypt and the Lord thy God redeemed thee." When he died, he left instructions that his epitaph read: "John Newton, clerk, once an infidel and libertine, a servant of slave in Africa, was by the mercy of our Lord and Saviour Jesus Christ preserved, restored, pardoned and appointed to preach the faith he had so long labored to destroy." Newton never forgot that amazing grace.

Grace? For *us?*

We are like that vagrant found frozen to death in a field during the winter of 1985 in northern New Jersey. He had seventy-five thousand dollars worth of uncashed checks and negotiable securities in his pockets and a plastic bag containing another thirty-five thousand dollars in certificates and bonds in his arms. All that wealth, but apparently the hapless man didn't know what to do with it. We have the news of Jesus Christ, yet we are not sure what to do about it. We don't know what His grace means.

Jesus comes to you where you are because He knows that you are not able to rise to where you want to be, to where you know you should be. He comes to you not where you ought to be, but where you *are.* "Just as I am," as the old hymn says it, He comes to you. Every saint has a past, and every sinner has a future, with and through the power of the risen Lord!

The Apostle Paul had a past. He acknowledged it, dubbing

himself the foremost of sinners. He carried no illusions about himself. He emphasized that he could be so open about it because he was forgiven. He was certain of his forgiveness in spite of his bleak and brutal past, in which he says ". . . I formerly blasphemed and persecuted and insulted him; but I received mercy . . ." (1 Timothy 1:13).

In Paul's correspondence, the words tumble forth in a cataract of thanks and praise. Paul states that in spite of those sorry occasions, the memories of which threatened to destroy him, Jesus Christ *strengthened* him, Jesus Christ *trusted* him, Jesus Christ *appointed* him for work.

Paul solemnly states, "The saying is sure and worthy of full acceptance, that Christ Jesus came into the world to save sinners . . ." (1 Timothy 1:15). The introductory words are the formal terminology used in a citation, and also the first words leading into the prayer used in all Jewish worship after the recitation of the *Shema*, as well as in Greek literary inscriptions. Paul used the most serious words he could find to tell everyone that God had restored the relationship between Himself and Paul through Jesus Christ. God in His mercy has accepted a man with a past. Sinner? Yes. But a sinner with a future!

You have a past. Accept it. Place that past in Christ's hands. Allow Him to love you into life. Deal with that past in the only way possible for living and not destroying yourself: Accept the Good News that through Jesus Christ God strengthens, trusts and appoints you. His amazing grace extends to you. Then carry out Christ's purpose by being His representative of mercy to those dying for want of hope and healing.

We are all guilt-ridden, and we are often depressed and angry and paralyzed. We punish ourselves. Jesus asks us: Why are you so hard on yourself? Why can you not be gentle with yourself?

Are you one of those who cannot seem to relax? Who will

not take a vacation or time off? Who worries and works nights, neglects family, is isolated from subordinates? Who cannot play and feels that play must be strenuous work if you do take time off? Who is overanxious about money? You no longer need to punish yourself. You need make no payment. You don't have to prove that you are acceptable. Jesus Christ has already accepted you!

Jesus never aroused a sense of guilt. He aroused a genuine awareness of sin, but He never harped on past mistakes or labeled another, "Sinner." He freely accepted even the worst and guiltiest.

Do you understand the Good News? All guilt trips canceled permanently by order of the Creator who has come in mercy through Jesus Christ! This is the significance of Jesus in your life, and is why Jesus is the Good News. You no longer need to trouble yourself or others with guilt-trip tickets.

But there is more.

God's amazing grace to you is not only to rescue you from the dungeon of guilt but also to appoint you to bear the hammer of mercy.

The Apostle Paul puts it in his usual pithy way: "but I received mercy for this reason, that in me, as the foremost, Jesus Christ might display his perfect patience for an example to those who were to believe in him for eternal life" (1 Timothy 1:16). In effect Paul says, "Amazing grace? To me? Why, Lord, to me?" Then he answers his own question: "To let others see God's goodness in Jesus Christ! To be an *example.*"

You are given amazing grace in order to be God's example to others as to what Jesus Christ can do. You are the crude working drawing of what the Designer has in mind for everyone. You have been given mercy to demonstrate mercy! Showing grace in your life is God's way of demonstrating, "Now *here's* what I have in mind!" You may be only a couple

of rough lines as a hint, but it is a fast look at what Jesus
Christ does and can do.

People may sometimes criticize you for not being Christ-
like enough. True, you're not. But if they saw you without
Jesus, they'd realize how much His grace applies!

16

Sustained in the Midst of Pressure

A cartoon in the *New Yorker* shows a man sitting at a desk looking anxiously at five barometers on the nearby wall. One barometer is lettered Job Pressure. Another states Financial Pressure. Still another reads Family Pressure. A fourth barometer carries the caption Time Pressure. The last is labeled Social Pressure. The cartoon brings a knowing smile to the viewer. No one needs those five barometers to remind him of severe daily pressures.

Pressure seems so pervasive in our world that even the animals are affected. The Tokyo zoo is now closed for two days each month because the animals were showing signs of ex-

treme stress. The strain of going public was getting them
down.   ▶

Nurses in blood-donor programs report an extraordinary
number of young executive types and spouses are rejected as
donors because of the high concentration of stress-reducing
chemicals in their blood. "You wouldn't believe the number
we have to turn down because they're on medication for
pressure-related problems such as hypertension, migraines,
depression, insomnia and high blood pressure," reports the
head of our local blood bank.

Americans gulped an average of seventy-seven aspirins per
person last year, according to Duke University Medical Center researchers. How many people can you list who cannot
make it through the day without drugs or alcohol?

Everyone lives under stress conditions. According to the
president's commission on mental health, one out of four is
under the kind of emotional stress that results in symptoms of
depression and anxiety.

Some, of course, are in jobs which are well-known pressure
cookers. Anyone in sports, for example, suffers from stress.
Lou Piniella of the Yankees struck out one time and, under
the stress of fanning again, struck out at the team's 100-cup
coffee maker.

Policemen, air-traffic controllers and firemen must live
under severe stress, and the tensions of constantly dealing
with life-and-death scenarios drive many into alcohol or drug
abuse. Their wives also suffer acutely from symptoms of
stress. Operating room nurses who must appear constantly
cool and composed, especially during pressure-packed hours
in surgery, complain of never being able to show a human
side.

Salesmen must cope with stress daily. Brokers find that as
the Dow Jones goes down, stress goes up. School administra-
tors, especially college and university presidents, have an average of about five years on the job before being turned out

by what is euphemistically called "administrative fatigue."

One group rarely discussed or studied that experiences exceptional stress is the working mother, especially in the single-parent home. Guilt, anxiety, self-depreciation, work overload and conflicting demands place such a woman in constant triple or quadruple binds.

Yuppies—young urban professionals—have been found to suffer acutely from pressure. Determined to do everything well and stay on the white-collar fast track, these young persons are frequently classic examples of burnout. They feel peer pressure to acquire the symbols of success. They are determined to make it earlier and are willing to work harder for it. Workaholism seems to be assumed. Superachievers professionally and socially, they are sometimes superfailures personally and spiritually. The pressures of holding onto the job grow: "I know that there are twelve of me in my office just waiting for my job," one young professional woman told a counselor.

Historians and anthropologists point out that humans have been living with stress since the beginning. Studies of skulls from ancient cultures show crude surgical efforts to relieve pressure pains in the head.

The Greeks had a word the Apostle Paul and other New Testament writers liked to use. The word is *thlipsis*. It is usually translated "affliction" or sometimes "suffering." These are flabby expressions of what the Greek word *thlipsis* means, since it really refers to being pressed down, squeezed by severe pressures. Sometimes in the punishing of criminals or torturing suspects, heavy weights were put on a person's chest or head, threatening to crush the person. That is *thlipsis*. Paul reports the kind of stress he had been experiencing by stating, " . . . we were so utterly, unbearably crushed that we despaired of life itself. Why, we felt that we had received the sentence of death . . ." (2 Corinthians 1:8, 9).

Haven't you felt that way? Have pressures in your life ever

threatened to squeeze the very life out of you? What about
tension headaches that cause you to gasp, "My head is split-
ting with pressure," or the pressures that make you feel the
heaviness in your chest?

"I have daggers sticking out all over my back," reports one
man who spends his working hours in a situation where corporation politics and office power plays have sapped his energies and ambitions for his department.

"I feel pressures in all my relationships," reports one working wife. "Tensions with my boss, tensions with my husband
and children, tensions with the others in the office, tension
with my clients, even certain tensions when we go out with
friends." She paused and added, "And I guess I feel a certain
tension about myself."

A recent survey reported that eight out of ten Americans
cite the need for less stress in their lives. Those surveyed
claimed it is harder to cope with the problems of daily living
now than it was a few years ago. Just making it through the
week is a stress-filled existence. The sources most often given
are inflation, fear of violence and personal safety, and the
pressures of trying to juggle family and job demands and
problems.

The same survey indicated that stress prevented most from
practicing good health habits, so that smoking, drinking and
eating were taking a destructive toll. Furthermore, those re-
plying said they knew that stress was lowering their own
sense of motivation or willpower in dealing meaningfully
with pressures. Marital problems, temper outbursts, anxieties, boredom, fatigue, insomnia, drinking problems, and a
fatalism ("When you number's up, your number's up") were
shown to accompany pressure.

Our Reactions to Stress

Our immediate reaction is to look for ways to ease or remove the symptoms of stress. We want a quick fix. We turn

to chemical crutches. Liquor may help for a few hours, but the banjo strings of pressure are screwed even tighter when the drug wears off. Popping over-the-counter pills to reduce stress feelings may ease things briefly, but the practice primarily enriches the pharmaceutical industry.

Going bowling and playing golf are wholesome sports, but even if you spent most of your waking hours in the bowling alleys or on the golf course, you would sense that your problems are more than overwork and insufficient exercise. In fact, if you are the typical workaholic feeling pressure, you often turn your play into work. You feel under pressure to bowl all strikes or to shoot in the low seventies.

You may con yourself into thinking you can run from pressure. I know a couple that made three trips to Walt Disney World in one year to escape the pressures of managing a small business. "It's the one place we know where there are no pressures and everyone's always smiling and everything works smoothly," the wife assured me.

"Yes," added the husband, "that's where we want to be: somewhere where we won't have to deal with pressures." The problem is that their money runs low and they have to return home. Their fantasies cannot be maintained perpetually. Even the drug of travel wears off.

Some well-meaning persons counsel us to lower the causes of stress. There is nothing wrong with trying to eliminate pressure factors. Who doesn't want some of the weights lifted off his chest and head? Some of those efforts are commendable, such as courses in helping us get better organized, do better planning and find ways to stop trying to be a superman or bionic woman. Other attempts to remove the causes of stress turn out to be naive and simplistic, such as the young man with the large *No Nukes* T-shirt who assured me that all reasons for stress would be removed from our world if we shut down all nuclear power plants for good.

Still other experts on handling pressures urge you to leave

the stress scene for a tranquil setting: "A different job or a new career or another location will alleviate the pressure." I personally know some ex-engineers and accountants who have tried to become potters and poets on Vermont farms and the California coastline, but who are just as tense and uneasy in old blue jeans as they were in well-tailored, three-piece suits. They took their pressures with them.

True Comfort

Pressure, we see, is not so much external as internal. When we look at the New Testament's mentions of pressure, we quickly notice that nothing is said about trying to relieve the symptoms. Nothing is said about practicing relaxing techniques, or taking a vacation, or pouring a potion to narcoticize yourself, or giving yourself pep talks, or reading cheering literature, or finding yourself a new partner, or using any method of ameliorating the symptoms of stress. Nor does the New Testament comment on removing the causes.

The New Testament repeatedly speaks of the God who comforts. *Comfort* is another one of those English words that has completely lost its fizz through translation. Comfort to us implies mere solace. It has passive connotations. Comfort to us means crawling into bed and turning the electric blanket up to nine. Comfort means gulping an aspirin or two, receiving a pat on the hand by a nice old parson, or cuddling into Mommy's lap.

In actuality, the term for *comfort* in Greek literally means "called to the side of." Comfort really means a relationship with the Lord. Comfort stands for a friend who cares —namely the living Lord. Comfort is the gift of God's presence, or the coming of the Holy Spirit.

God introduces Jesus as the risen Lord to our midst. We are not alone. God does not tune us out. He does not put us on hold, then forget to get back to our calls. The Lord remembers us in our pain and loneliness, He fortifies us, strengthens us by standing with us, steadies us.

Before becoming a jet pilot in the Navy, a recruit is sent to Naval Aviation Officer Candidate School. Officer Candidate School is a grueling thirteen weeks of training that is designed to weed out those unfit for the physical and psychological demands of a naval officer. During these thirteen weeks, many candidates find themselves on the edge of D.O.R. (dropping out on request). Those who saw the film *An Officer and a Gentleman* will remember the tension between Sergeant Foley, the mean, tough drill instructor, and the recruits, in which the sergeant appears to delight in brutally pushing his recruits into D.O.R. Only great determination on the part of the young recruits to stand up to the nerve-straining tests enables them to keep alive their hopes of becoming officers and fliers.

We Christians are constantly pressured to the point of D.O.R. by the forces opposed to God. Tough and mean people and tough and mean circumstances try to force us to drop out of God's community and forsake our calling. However, we have comfort. The risen Lord sustains us in the midst of our pressure periods.

The living Lord braces us to stand up to the pressures to conform. Unfortunately, we often try to do what the culture around us calls us to do. We forget God's comfort. Listening to the crowd will cause us to miss God's way.

We will be like the man and his son described in an old story. The father and son were on their way to market with their donkey. At first, the man sat on the animal and the boy walked alongside. Then they heard people saying, "How terrible! Look at that strong man riding on the donkey and that poor little boy having to walk."

So the father got off and put the boy on the donkey. They continued farther, but heard other people saying, "Look at that lazy boy, sitting there on that donkey and making his poor father walk."

At this, the father got back on the donkey and they both rode. However, they saw people pointing at them and heard them say, "What cruel people, both of them sitting on one donkey."

So they both got off and walked alongside the donkey. They had not gone much farther when they heard some bystanders laughing and stating, "How silly! A healthy donkey with no one on its back, and those two people are walking!"

Embarrassed, the man and his boy picked up the donkey and started to carry it. They never did get to the market!

It is the little day-by-day pressures that wear us down most severely. The constant rubbing of pressure can work silent danger for the person not comforted by Christ.

On racing yachts, there are numerous dangers and problems not encountered in any other sport. The big seagoing sailing boats are sleek and beautiful when their sails are filled with wind. Few realize that these graceful craft are prone to what is known as chafe.

The crew constantly inspects for chafe, one of the biggest problems in long-distance sailing. Sails rub on the rigging, and worn spots have to be patched before the entire sails tear. Chafe also occurs on the wire halyards that are used to hoist and hold up the sails, and that can spell disaster if they break in a strong wind.

We humans find ourselves suffering from a type of chafe from the pressures, stress and wear of daily life. Life gets tough and threatens to break even the strongest person. There is good news, however, for everyone afflicted with chafe of the mind or spirit. Jesus Christ comes bringing renewed strength. With Him, we have new staying power. No matter how severely we are afflicted with tough storms in life, He stands by us, enabling us to cope!

Have you ever noticed that Jesus was almost constantly under pressure during His ministry? Every waking hour was occupied with teaching and healing. Controversy swirled around Him. People repeatedly interrupted His plans and upset His schedule. The opposition tightened its efforts to trap Him. The hour of sacrifice loomed closer. The disciples continued to be obtuse and unable to comprehend who He was or what His mission was. Throughout His entire pressure-packed ministry, however, Jesus was never ruffled. He never snapped irritably or lost His poise.

Take the occasion when one of the men who headed the opposition came up to Jesus. The man had to see Jesus immediately. It is urgent, he insists.

Some of the disciples grumble. "What's this man trying to pull on the Master now? Hasn't he done enough mischief?"

Agitated, the man finally gets to talk to Jesus. "It's my little girl," he gasps. "My only child ... she's terribly ill ... and they say she won't make it." Desperately, he pleads, "Would you come?"

Jesus could have found a dozen ways of brushing him off. He could have found another dozen ways of putting the man in his place. After all, why should the Master knock himself out for a man who has been making His life so miserable? Besides, Jesus needs rest; His schedule has been a killer.

But Jesus went with him. (*See* Mark 5:24.)

God, who has a hundred excuses for dusting off His hands, mumbling that He is fed up with humans and their stubborn disobedience, has chosen not to abandon us. In spite of every reason in the book for ignoring us, He pledges that He goes with us.

Martin Luther learned that Jesus Christ went with him through days of stress-filled events. Take, for example, the occasion when he had to travel to the city of Worms to face one of his worst ordeals. Pressures were mounting to silence him. Rumors were rife that hit squads would assassinate him. Luther entered Worms on April 16, 1521, amidst a popular demonstration. When he fell into bed that night, he was exhausted. The following day, in the afternoon, he was scheduled to appear before the Diet for a hearing. It was a time of immense stress. On the morning of the tense Diet, what did

Luther do? Did he frantically go over his notes, polishing his presentation to the authorities? No. Luther spent the morning visiting a dying person who had asked to have Luther call and pray. Luther entered the hall that afternoon and faced his accusers with a smile. That sense of poise in the midst of pressure is the secret of the Reformation!

Alfred Stocks knows that Jesus Christ steadies him by going with him to a place of pressure. Alfred Stocks serves as the city manager of the large English city of Liverpool. He faces immense pressures and near-impossible challenges. Liverpool is experiencing massive urban challenges. The population is declining. The old industries have left or are leaving. Widespread unemployment and a shrinking tax base cause serious financial problems. Once-respectable neighborhoods are declining. Racial tensions flared into several nights of riots and firebombings a few summers ago. Restless youth, unable to find work, are drifting into street crime. Alfred Stocks, however, is a Christian. He is also human. Stocks understands the meaning of pressure. He feels the pain of his fellow citizens and he accepts the hurts inflicted by angry critics. But Alfred Stocks maintains his equilibrium. He comments, "Before I get there in the morning, Jesus Christ is already in the office and there to meet me when I open the door." Stocks therefore goes to work with hope.

Go out into the Christian community in certain other countries. Meet some of the valiant believers who must live under unbelievable pressures. For starters, they are pressured almost daily to renounce their faith. In Nepal, they will possibly lose their jobs. In Pakistan, they may lose their seniority or opportunity for advancement. In North Korea, they will lose their freedom; in Vietnam or Cambodia, their life. In the Soviet Union, they may experience the dreaded knock on their door at midnight for being public about their faith.

Here, you do not have the danger of the lash, but of the laugh. You don't run the risk of jail, but of a jeer. You won't have to endure the pain of torture, but of teasing. But the risen One who stands in your midst also suffered—for you! And He calls you to take up whatever cross of risk and shame and pressure you may face, with the certainty that when you go public with the news that He is alive, He stands with you!

A few years ago in Illinois, carpenters were putting together a prefabricated house. Under pressure to set a record in assembling the building, they put it together so fast that one of the workmen was caught in it. They had to rip down a section to get him out.

In the pressure to throw together our lives, we have imprisoned our souls. We have often been so pressed to get on with building that we forget the person that God means us to be. Even saintly Rufus Jones, the great Quaker teacher and writer on the inner life, admitted that the pressures of life sometimes kept him from remembering who he was before God. "I live like leaves in constant whirl," he wrote once to his wife. "Hither and yon I go, always talking like a gab machine . . . I talk of quiet and hush and I praise concentration, but I rush about like a dervish and act as though the life here below were a dash from x to y—two unknown points."

On May 24, 1941, the British warship *Prince of Wales* sighted the Nazi battleship *Bismarck*. Captain Leach of the *Prince of Wales* and his crew felt under desperate pressure. They knew they would have to steam for another twenty minutes before they could get in close enough to open fire. Urgent last-minute preparations for shelling were made. Men stood tensely at their battle stations. The pressure of waiting grew. Then the captain remembered one thing they had not done. He summoned the chaplain, the Reverend W. G. Parker.

"Padre," asked Captain Leach, "can you remember a prayer which begins, 'O God, Thou knowest how busy I am . . . ?' "

"It is Sir Jacob Astley's prayer before the battle of Edgehill, Sir," answered the chaplain, "and I have the words in my cabin."

"Fetch it quickly. There's not much time."

Shortly, through the loudspeakers on the great ship, in the midst of the tension and pressures of a forthcoming battle, came the calm voice of Chaplain Parker. He read a prayer written for people in a different war in a different age, but those words spoke to the men enduring stress that fateful day in the South Atlantic.

"O Lord, Thou knowest how busy we must be today. If we forget Thee, do not Thou forget us; for Christ's sake. Amen."

Bring in a Candle

The most difficult thing in having to put up with pressure is wondering what the purpose of it is. Is there any meaning to the stress situations we are forced to endure? What's the point of the squeeze and pressure? We want to invest our suffering with some sense of purpose.

The New Testament does not reflect in detail on why we suffer from pressures. The writers did not spend time in speculating. Stress was one of the givens in life. They knew as Christians they could expect to be subjected to terrible pressures. They did not write articles analyzing the causes of stress, or discourse on the philosophical reasons for pressures. They knew that stress threatened to squeeze them in its gruesome coils. They also realized their readers would be subjected to cruel pressures. The weights were on their chests and heads; *thlipsis* tortured them.

The New Testament fairly sings with hope and confidence, however, when it states that the risen Lord is at your side. Jesus offers a sufficient answer to stress screams from any believer: If you want a sense of purpose for experiencing pressures, use your knowledge of Jesus Christ's comforting, enlivening, energizing presence to be a comfort to others. He is the Helper. You are to be a mini-comfort, a replica of His kind of help for others.

Everyone around you is signaling for someone to fortify him, to stand as one called to his side. "Does anyone really care whether I live or die?" whisper those near you.

Or, as another confided, "Secretly I feel life is out of control and I'm just one more unremembered passenger on a world that's plunging in an irreversible dive. I can't do much. I don't count for much."

This sense of futility and helplessness, loneliness and fear is what so many around us feel. A few of us, Christ's people, know differently. We have received strength. From now on, our stress-filled lives will be used to steady those around us and to mobilize them for action.

In 1789, in the Connecticut legislature, pressures were exacting a toll. The young republic was trying to recover from a long, costly struggle for independence. Former separate colonies were grappling with problems of fledgling states united to other states. Individuals were tired of sacrifices. Prices were soaring. Taxes were a burden. Economic conditions were worsening.

One day, as the Connecticut legislators sat at work, the sky darkened. The sun's light was obscured. It was too much for some. Frightened people whispered that the end of the world and the Second Coming were at hand. Some started to prepare to flee to the hills. Others resigned themselves to inaction. Then a certain Colonel Davenport stood and spoke. "The Day of Judgment is either approaching or it is not. If it is not, there is no cause for adjournment. But if it is, I wish to be found doing my duty. I wish therefore that candles be brought."

Let candles be brought in! Steady and strengthen those around you who are unsteady and weak from not having anyone called to their side!

17

Believe, That You May Understand

The explorer Alexander Mackenzie trudged for years across the Canadian Northwest, thinking he would discover an opening to the Pacific Ocean. He finally came across a river and followed its long course for miles. Instead of coming upon the shore of the Pacific, however, the river led him to the icy coast of the Arctic Ocean. He named the stream he had followed for so many weeks The River of Disappointment. Facing the facts that he could not change either the geography of the northwestern wilds of Canada or his own diminishing strength, he plodded back to civilization.

There are some things in life that apparently cannot be

changed. Mackenzie, like many of us, started out on a thrilling quest, anticipating victories and confident of accomplishing much. Instead he encountered things he could not change.

Every person discovers that certain rivers trail into frozen wasteland.

Of course, you can rail and complain because there are things in life you cannot change. In 1752, after 170 years of resisting the Gregorian calendar, the British finally realized they weren't going to change the rest of the world's way of figuring the dates on the calendar. Switching to the new style calendar put the British in sync with Europe and every other western nation. The new calendar, however, did not sit well with many British. It caused complications in business dealings and church holy days. Angry protests broke out. Many stubbornly refused to accept the Gregorian calendar and defiantly tried to continue with the old. Numerous Britons grumbled for years over having to accept a parliamentary act they could not change.

Needless to say, there are some things in life that we *think* we cannot change, but which turn out otherwise.

Many years ago, an eastern bishop paid his annual visit to a small midwestern religious college. He stayed at the home of the young, progressive president, who also served as professor of physics and chemistry. After dinner, the faculty gathered to meet with the bishop. The bishop discoursed on how the Millennium could not be far off because he was sure that, among other signs, everything about nature had been discovered and all inventions had been conceived.

The young college president politely disagreed and said he felt that within the coming fifty years, there would be many more discoveries. The bishop was angered by this and challenged the president to name just one invention of the future. The president replied that he was certain that within fifty years, men would be able to fly. "Nonsense! Only angels are intended to fly," sputtered the outraged bishop.

The bishop's name was Wright. He had two boys at home, Orville and Wilbur.

Even when some things in life do change later, before those changes come, we deplore and despair.

"Not in the lifetime of most men has there been so much grave and deep apprehension.... The domestic economic situation is in chaos. Our dollar is weak throughout the world. Prices are so high as to be utterly impossible.... Of our troubles no man can see the end."

Is this an editorial from this morning's newspaper or comments by a national figure on the news last night? Actually, the quotation above appeared in *Harper's Weekly* in October, 1857—over a century ago!

Even John Calvin grew weary when it seemed he had to face situations in Geneva that would never change. "The future appalls me," moaned Calvin. "I dare not think of it; unless the Lord descends from heaven, barbarism will engulf us."

On Decmeber 17, 1547, he wrote to Viret: "I hardly hope that the Church can be upheld much longer, at least by my ministry. Believe me, my power is broken, unless God stretch forth His Hand."

The Faith Factor

Is God a petty-minded accountant who remembers every slight and injury, who arranges to settle His grudges by inflicting things we cannot change? Does God test us? Is He a brutal coach who intends to toughen us up so we can "take it"? Is this universe, as George Bernard Shaw once sarcastically wrote, "a moral gymnasium built expressly to strengthen your character in"? Does God, the unmoved, unmovable mover, plot pain to tell us that we are weak and useless compared to Him? Does He in his impassive and detached aloofness arrange for us to suffer, just to remind us that He can do as He pleases?

God is not like a cruel boy maiming birds and crippling animals to watch their reactions. Only a psychotic intentionally tortures others. In Jesus, our God stated, "I am come that you might have life!" (see John 10:10). God comes as Savior, not as sadist.

Having to face things you cannot change does not mean God is angrily retaliating for insults and injuries. Rather than punish, He pities: "As a father pities his children, so the Lord pities those who fear him" (Psalms 103:13).

Trusting Him, we understand that He stands as Redeemer and Friend.

It may well be that we will still have questions, but because of Jesus Christ, we will be able to put our questions in proper perspective. As Augustine, who painfully learned that faith must precede understanding, said, "Seek not to understand that you may believe, but believe that you may understand!"

William Booth knew this. Booth, a dedicated apostle to the forgotten millions in nineteenth-century English slums, underwent a serious eye operation in the midst of his busy, useful ministry. Doctors had Booth's son, Bramwell, tell the doughty founder of the Salvation Army that he would probably be blind the rest of his life. When he heard the news, General Booth calmly answered, "I have done what I could for God and the people with my eyes. Now I shall do for God and the people what I can without my eyes."

The faith factor is paramount in facing things that cannot be changed. One of the most extraordinary things to come out of the Korean War was how poorly many young American soldiers stood up to privations. One staggering story reported the situation in a large prisoner-of-war camp. A large number of the men captured were very young soldiers, still in their teens. Physically they were healthy and tough when captured. They certainly seemed destined to survive. Yet, these young, hardy, healthy teenage G.I.s died off by the dozens.

In one particular camp, there were not only large numbers

of teenage soldiers, but also a contingent of Roman Catholic sisters. These nuns were all in their sixties, all frail. Everyone in that camp received exactly the same food and medical care. Surprisingly, it was the youngsters who gave up and died, while every one of the nuns survived.

General Maxwell Taylor concluded that there was only one thing that spelled the difference between those who survived and those who died: *Faith.*

Christians persevere in living, even in the face of enduring those things that cannot be changed. Christian faith is, among other things, an attitude of "I am determined to do my duty regardless of what happens."

God Works for Good

We Christians have a sense of history and remember that there have been times of dark ages. Of all people, we are the hard-nosed realists, knowing that humans can and do cause infernal disorder to God's design. But we also take comfort in the Resurrection. It's no accident that in St. Pierre's Church, where Calvin preached in Geneva, these words are inscribed on the wall: *Post Tenebrae, Lux* (After darkness, Light!).

God raised up Jesus Christ alive. He lives. With Him, through Him and for Him, we can face any apparently unchangeable situation. We know that God always ultimately prevails.

The cause of the Reformation seemed lost in Scotland in 1559. Powerful forces opposed John Knox. The affairs of the fledgling reformed church in Scotland caused many churchmen to despair, but not Knox! With words of unusual conviction and hope, he courageously stated, "Yea, whatsoever may become of us and our mortal carcasses, I doubt not but this cause (in spite of Satan) shall prevail in the realm of Scotland. For as it is the eternal truth of the Eternal God, so shall it once prevail howsoever for a time it be impugned."

We can look all the tragedy, darkness, suffering and evil in the face. We are not struck hopeless. We are energized by

God, knowing that in everything, God works for good with those who love Him. When we love God, we know He cooperates in all respects for good.

This is what Paul learned. Life was not easy. God did not "pay off." Paul had a meager living. He knew hardships—stoning, shipwreck, hunger, cold. He took criticism, opposition, and disappointments. Suffering long imprisonment, he hardly knew anything working out for "good," as we'd say.

Because he knew that God could not be hemmed in, Paul never felt he was trapped. Rotting in that Roman jail or being beheaded by the executioner—Paul could face either because of what God did at the cross and Resurrection. ". . . I am put here . . ." (Philippians 1:16) Paul writes. It is a military phrase: "I am posted here"—*assigned, placed, appointed* to this position.

In effect, Paul says, "So I may have to be in these circumstances where nothing can change, but I can look upon it now as the place where I happen to be at the moment on the battle line. Not pleasant or safe, but where I happen to be. Therefore, I'll look upon it as a post under God for the time being."

". . . what has happened to me has really served to advance the gospel" (Philippians 1:12). Paul uses another military expression: To *advance* is the word to describe the movement of an army or expedition where scouts hack away the underbrush, chop away obstructions, remove barriers, clear away anything hindering progress.

In other words, Paul's imprisonment is anything but a dead end. It is actually a means of clearing away hindrances to the advance of the Gospel!

The apostle even gives examples. He is able to preach to a group never touched before by the Church—the Praetorian Guard, the elite corps of handpicked troops, the ten thousand crack troopers in the emperor's bodyguard. Paul was chained day and night for a time to one of these guards and met frequently with groups of soldiers in the prison.

Paul was not delivered *from* prison. Paul was delivered *in* prison. He was able to witness to God's goodness through his letters. He held conversations with guards, talks with visitors. Sustained by God, Paul was aware of the comfort, grace, and purpose of God.

This is what a pastor in East Germany learned not too long ago. He came to his church's central headquarters with a problem. He was threatened with prison on a trumped-up charge that would ruin his reputation unless he became an informer for the secret police.

"This is serious problem; we shall discuss it and advise you later," replied church headquarters. When the advice came, it was no longer necessary.

"Never mind, God has given me an answer," the pastor said. "If He takes away this congregation in Lower Apfelburg from me, He will give me another one—in Siberia."

With those who love God, He cooperates in all respects for good. This is true in your life as well, when you trust, love and obey Him. This promise is not based on some feeling produced by a worship service or by some pep talk by a preacher. This is not based on some rose-colored-glasses view of life, some phony keep-smiling optimism. This is the working of the God who even took a cross and turned it into the symbol of life, hope and forgiveness. This same God lives and rules now. He works in everything for good with those who love Him now.

Young Carl Bates was known as a tough cookie. He drank heavily. When he wasn't drinking in a bar, he was gambling in sleazy casinos. He drifted from city to city, becoming more deeply discouraged with himself and his life. Nothing would ever change for him, he cynically concluded.

One night in a New Orleans hotel, he decided he would end his life. He was fed up with everything, especially the emptiness in his own existence, and opened the window preparing to jump to his death. As he stood by the open window, gazing at the street below, he tried to muster the courage to leap. At that moment, he noticed a Gideon Bible in the hotel room.

"I was a self-styled agnostic," Bates later confessed, "but as I read that Bible, it dawned on me that I had cut myself off from God."

Carl Bates continued reading. He closed the window and did not kill himself. Instead, he discovered that Jesus Christ raised him from the death of anger and despair.

The resurrected Carl began a career that led him to study for the ministry. Later, as the Reverend Dr. Carl E. Bates, he accepted the post of president of the Southern Baptist Convention, America's largest Protestant denomination.

The resurrection of Carl Bates one night in 1934 in a lonely hotel room in New Orleans is but one of millions of times the risen, living Jesus Christ has raised up those in despair over facing things that cannot be changed.

Adoniram Judson, God's messenger in Burma, prayed to God to go to India. Instead, he went to Burma. He prayed for his wife's life, but buried her and his two children. He prayed for release from confinement in a steaming, filthy Oriental prison, but laid there in chains for months. Yet at the close of his life the great Baptist missionary stated, "I never prayed sincerely and earnestly for anything but it came; at some time—no matter how distant a day—somehow—in some shape—probably the last I should have devised—it came."

Christ's friends know that their prayers will sustain them in times of facing things that cannot be changed. William Law, one of the great eighteenth-century men of faith, wrote, "If anyone would tell you the shortest, surest way to all happiness and all perfection, he must tell you to make a rule to yourself to thank and praise God for everything that happens to you. For it is certain that whatever seeming calamity happens to you, if you thank and praise God for it, you turn it into a blessing . . . [the true saint] is not he who prays most or fasts most . . . who gives alms most or is most eminent for temperance . . . or justice; but it is he who is always thankful to God, who wills everything that God wills, who receives everything as an instance of God's goodness, and has a heart always ready to praise God for it."

In the midst of circumstances that cannot be changed, God's love will not let us go. Even in the unchangeable circumstances of declining health and approaching death.

Helen Keller, left totally blind and deaf because of illness, lived almost her entire life in a dark, silent world. Nevertheless, she grew to be a sensitive, educated person who made a profound contribution to American life in the first half of the twentieth century. Speaking about life and death in her old age, Miss Keller, a deeply committed Christian, said: "There's still so much I'd like to see, so much to learn. And death is just around the corner. Not that that worries me. On the contrary, it is no more than passing from one room into another. But there's a difference for me, you know. Because in that other room I shall be able to see."

You die pretty much as you live. Your attitude toward facing death must be fashioned before the showdown with death comes, and your attitude comes from how you relate to the One who is the Resurrection and the life.

John Wesley, founder of the Methodist Church, was a person who knew the Lord of life and death, and who could therefore face anything. Once Wesley was asked how he would spend his time if he knew he would die by midnight the next day. Wesley confidently answered, "Why just as I had expected to spend the time. I would preach at Gloucester tonight and tomorrow morning, at Tewkesbury in the afternoon, go to my friend Martin's house for entertainment, converse and pray with the family as usual, retire to my room at ten o'clock, commend myself to my heavenly Father, lie down to rest, and wake up in glory."

Could you say something like this in the face of circumstances you cannot change?

18

A New Creation

You are thirty-five going on seventy. The mirror shows the gray hairs, the wrinkles and the bulges, and your lower-back pains send signals that your frame is not the same. You empathize with tennis champ Rod Laver commenting on his attempt to play in an exhibition match after his retirement, "Sometimes my poor old body can't get there."

It's more than shortness of breath when you try to race up the steps. It's also calculating that you have already lived roughly half of your life. You realize that you will not fulfill all the aspirations of your youth. Earlier, you could jolly yourself along with the notion that with enough sweat, guts and grit, you could climb to the top. Now you are forced to acknowledge that you have pretty much done what you are capable of doing and will probably have to keep on doing it. You are in a holding pattern. You see yourself not so much on a ladder leading upward as on a treadmill leading to the golden handshake. The Yuppies, ever younger and brighter and peppier, are pushing to pass you.

Do you recall the lines in *The Autumn Garden* by Lillian Hellman, where Griggs admits, "That big hour of decision, the turning point in your life, the someday you'd counted on when you'd suddenly wipe out your past mistakes, do the work you'd never done, think the way you'd never thought, have what you'd never had—it just doesn't come suddenly. You've trained yourself for it while you waited—or you've let it all run past you and frittered yourself away. I've frittered myself away."

This is the discovery of middle age. This is the time when free-floating anxiety seems to seep into a person's bones. Eric Berne in *Games People Play* calls it the time when people play "Balance Sheet." This is the period of stocktaking. Sometimes, it is an agonizing reappraisal and you discover how little your achievements measure up to your goals and values. If you are a woman, you may be drifting into a crisis of purposelessness. Life means face lifts, hair tints, quack diets and forever gazing over a sea of bridge tables.

Paging through her high-school yearbook in anticipation of her twenty-fifth reunion, one woman reflected on how the eighteen-year-old pom-pom girl who bore her name and filled her skin had actually not occupied the premises for quite a while, although she sometimes feels her stir inside.

If you are a man, you are conscious of the youth cult in the United States where to turn twenty-five is to pass the outer limits of human obsolescence. You are in the age bracket where alcoholism climbs a steep 50 percent, where the medicine chests start to look like drugstores, where there is the temptation to have an affair with a young girl.

One man privately admitted to me, "For me the world stopped in August, 1945. Everything after the war has been an

anticlimax. Nothing important, nothing interesting has happened to me since then. I've been plodding through an end-
less swamp, it seems, since then."

Popular psychological jargon such as "mid-life crisis" has
come into our vocabulary, and with it a lot of fatuous advice.
Mouthing the clichés, some try to relocate the machinery by
changing jobs, changing mates, changing careers. The sense
of growing older is the realization that you're stuck with it—
career, job, residence, status, family or whatever—for the
rest of your life. And this is the period when insomnia, depression, drinking problems, marital squabbling, infidelity,
divorce, and psychosomatic ailments flourish.

You may try to stop the calendar by a superficial change,
but what you are trying to rinse out of your hair is actually
called Dorian Grey. True, Dorian Grey never grew old. His
tragedy was that he never grew! Trying to halt time, he
merely stunted his self.

The stunted self of one not wanting to admit to feeling
older imagines that license is freedom, that whims are tastes,
that movement is progress, that busyness is deeds. This is
merely a middle-aged kid trying to deny his or her age.

Contrast this notion with the attitude expressed by Adlai
Stevenson: "What a man knows at fifty that he did not know
at twenty boils down to something like this: The knowledge
that he has acquired with age is not the knowledge of for-
mulas, or forms of words, but of people, places, actions—a
knowledge not gained by words but by touch, sight, sound,
victories, failures, sleeplessness, devotion, love—the human
experiences and emotions of this earth; and perhaps, too, a
little faith and a little reverence for the things you cannot
see."

How do you get this knowledge?

Not by telling yourself, "Face up to life and learn to live
with gray hair and a sore back." Not by getting a new hobby
or going back to school. You need a relationship with God.
You need a rebirth, a conversion. Unless you have a vital and

growing faith, your latent neuroses will take over. The truth is that there are no neuroses in middle age which are not latent earlier!

Furthermore, old age does not bring any magic release or change. In fact, it only accentuates what you already are. If you are a quarrelsome, angry, fretful middle-aged person, you will be even more of a quarrelsome, angry, fretful elderly person. Your creativity will have soured even more into neuroses. Only an awakening, a new beginning, can deliver you.

Without Jesus Christ to guide us to maturity, we seem to find ourselves restless and driven. Our fame and fortunes do not seem to be able to help us to cope or to grow. Jesus Christ is our true guide to mature living.

Have you ever gone to your car on a winter morning and discovered that you had a flat tire due to a slow leak? You probably noticed the tire was low the day before and intended to have it fixed. But now, at 7:00 A.M. with an appointment to keep, you realize that yesterday's intentions mean nothing. You almost wish you could have had a blowout yesterday, so you would have had to get the tire repaired.

Our faith seldom gives out in a blowout. We usually lose it gradually in the middle years due to a slow leak. We tell ourselves, "I went to Sunday school and church every week as a child, but when I left home, I just got too busy for that sort of thing." Or we excuse our lack of praying with stories of how pious our parents were. Or we think we have been granted a sort of honorable discharge from Christian service. "We used to be very active in our old church: taught a class; sang in the choir; helped in the stewardship campaigns; served on the board. But since moving here, we just haven't got around to worshipping anywhere."

Faith must be renewed! Especially during the middle years.

In a church in London, a bronze tablet carries the words, "Here God laid His hands on William Booth." One day, a man entered that church and stood a long time in front of that bronze tablet. The time came when the church was to be closed for the day, and the caretaker walked up to the man. The man begged for another minute. The caretaker impatiently stood aside. As he waited, he overheard the man praying. The man pleaded, "O God, do it again!" The man was William Booth.

God has laid His hands on you. Do you remember? Perhaps it was years ago. Perhaps it was recently. Pray daily. Pray, "O Lord, do it again!" Read the Bible. Study it as God's message to you. Listen to the voice of the Spirit through the words of Scripture.

Don't look for gimmicks. Don't ask for shortcuts. Beware of those who offer neatly packaged tricks to make the Bible easy. These almost always end by substituting human wisdom for God's Word. Paul warned, ". . . we refuse to practice cunning or to tamper with God's word . . ." (2 Corinthians 4:2).

Let's talk about your commitment as a Christian. Are you dedicating yourself again to the Lord each day? Are you growing in your own faith? Growing in faith is answering daily the whispers and nudges of the Spirit. Faith is never static; it is always in process. One does not have faith like having brown eyes or gray hair, nor does one possess faith like holding shares of stock bequeathed by a rich uncle. Faith is responding to God's goodness and nearness in the person of Jesus Christ, through the Holy Spirit.

With a growing faith, you can face all aspects of growing older, including retirement.

"The day I retired," one man told me, "I felt like I went through a one hundred percent markdown."

Contrast this dismal comment with the reply of Arthur John Gossip. Gossip had lived a productive life as a professor at Glasgow University. Friends, concerned that he would grow depressed after leaving his busy academic career, asked what he would do after he retired. "What will I do after I retire?" Gossip answered. "Why, man, keep on living till I'm dead." Those who knew A. J. Gossip knew that by "living," he meant trusting Christ and serving Him in every way possible.

The person of faith, knowing it's his duty to *live* as he can, learns that he can also cope with declining health. Growing older means physical limitations, but these do not limit faith or creativity.

Robert Louis Stevenson radiated faith in spite of health problems most of his life. Afflicted with tuberculosis, he nevertheless continued his prodigious literary output. His right hand grew crippled, preventing him from writing, so he taught himself to write with his left. When both hands gave out, he dictated his writings. Finally his voice failed. Even that handicap did not stall Stevenson. He learned to use sign language to produce another novel. Ravaged by tuberculosis, he died at forty-four. Shortly before his death, however, buoyed by his faith, he dictated through sign language, "This world is so full of a number of things. I am sure we should all be as happy as kings."

There is strong evidence that age is no barrier for creativity. Michelangelo carved his immortal *Pieta* at seventy-five. At eighty-one, he painted the dome of St. Peter's, and at eighty-nine worked on his magnificent canvasses and continued as chief architect of St. Peter's basilica. At eighty-three, Toscanini was still conducting symphony orchestras. Goethe wrote *Faust*, his masterpiece, at eighty-two. Tennyson was eighty-three when he composed his great poem "Crossing the Bar." Ben Franklin at seventy-seven sailed to Paris to serve his country, and at eighty-one worked diligently at the Constitutional Convention. Gladstone was elected prime minister for the fourth time at eighty-three. In their seventies and eighties, Charles de Gaulle and Konrad Adenauer led France and Germany respectively, and at seventy-four Ronald Reagan began his second term as president. To be old does not mean being useless.

An ancient tale from the Middle East relates how a caliph traveled along an old road and noticed an elderly man planting olive trees. Knowing that olive trees require years and years to mature before they produce fruit, the surprised caliph asked the old man why he bothered to plant olive trees. "You will not live to see the fruits of your labors," said the caliph.

"Yes, that is true," answered the wise old man. "I will not live to eat any of the olives from these trees. But others planted so that we should eat. Therefore, we must plant so that those to come shall eat."

Others have played an important role in our lives, some being instrumental in the way our faith has been shaped. We, in turn, are called to plant and cultivate so that others may eat, so that children and future generations will be nurtured physically, spiritually, and socially. When we have faith, we will use our creativity for others.

Eventually, of course, the enemy, time, seems to tyrannize. Life has always been bounded by horizons, but time brutalizes us with the final horizon. Whether life seems hopelessly long or hopelessly short, time is the enemy.

God is not subject to time; God is independent of time. God, the eternal, came *into* time. God invaded the calendar, breaking through into the hours-and-days world we know.

God came into this life of change and allowed Himself to experience the onslaught of the enemy, time. Because of Him, through Him, we find our years are given a new dimension: God in Christ gives us "newness of life."

While we are young, we entertain the delusion that author William Saroyan stated a few days before his death in 1981: "Everybody has got to die, but I have always believed an exception would be made in my case." Older and wiser now, we are not so self-assured. Secretly, we think that the end of our lives is the end of history. We assume it all ends when we die. We assume that when we die, even God goes out of business.

The anxiety of death is not so much the pain or actual experience of dying. Rather, it is the question, "Will there be a time when I shall be forgotten? Eventually, will I become forgotten forever?" The anxiety that you or I will be forgotten both now and in eternity is the worst of death's sting.

We all resist being pushed into the past, to being relegated to memories. Remember the first time you returned to the campus where you once felt so happy and part of things, or back to your hometown, or the place you had once worked? This is a slight intimation of being buried. Being buried is being forgotten, being removed from the realm of awareness, being taken from the surface of the earth. Burial is the anxiety of being forever forgotten. Will there be any who remember? What about when they die? And what about all those worthwhile things we want to have remembered, which no one will bother remembering?

Death is the final humiliation, the ultimate seal of failure. We say that in the midst of life we die.

God answers: *In the midst of death, you are raised to life!*

In Jesus Christ, God has caused the death of death. That strange line in the Apostles' Creed, "He descended into hell," may puzzle us. Jesus faced the enemy, death. He suffered all the dread and horror of dying, but He was raised to a newness of life. He stands saying, "Because I live, you shall live also!" He is raising us to newness of life. Through that same risen, living Jesus Christ, God gives life to the dead. He reaches into the hollowness of nonexistence and gives life. The Creator makes a new creation, and this is what He is already at work doing in you and me.

The old Bill Barker used to fight a losing battle against that conquering tyrant, time. The old Barker used to wage a hopeless fight against despair, guilt, selfishness. The old Barker used to try to put up a brave front against death. But Barker lost. He lost completely. Time and sin and death beat Barker—beat him decisively and overwhelmingly.

That Barker died. And so did you. You and I really died at
baptism, when we were made Christ's. In a sense, our deaths
took place some 1900 years ago on Calvary. For when Christ
died, the old "me" died!

You and I have already gone through death. The events
that will take place someday in a hospital or on a highway or
battlefield mean little. These are minor footnotes to our
stories. The big news is that God has raised us to new life and
promises us resurrection!

Time and death no longer control us. They have already
tried to do their worst—and lost. What philosopher Martin
Heidegger called the "iron ring around existence" has been
broken by God's mighty act at the first Easter!

God is Lord of life and death, time and eternity. When
Episcopal Bishop Warren Chandler was faced with death, he
was asked, "Do you dread to cross the river of death?" He replied, "My Father owns the land on both sides of the river.
Why should I fear?"

The resurrection of Jesus Christ assures us that we are also
made alive in new ways by the God who cares for us. The
risen One is God's way of telling us that He has known us
from eternity. The living Lord promises that God remembers
us always and constantly! Forever!

"Let not your hearts be troubled. . . . because I live, you
will live also" (John 14:1, 19).